I'm Retiring, Now What?!™

by Hope Egan and Barbara Wagner

SILVER
LINING
BOOKS
NEW YORK

For information contact:
Silver Lining Books
122 Fifth Avenue
New York, NY 10011

First Edition
This edition was published by Silver Lining Books.

Printed and Bound in the United States of America

Other titles in the Now What?!™ series:

I'm turning on my PC, Now What?!
I'm turning on my iMac, Now What?!
I'm in the Wine Store, Now What?!
I'm in the Kitchen, Now What?!
I need to get in Shape, Now What?!
I need a Job, Now What?!
I haven't saved a Dime, Now What?!
I'm on the Internet, Now What?!
I just bought a Digital Camera, Now What?!
I'm getting Married, Now What?!

introduction

"I can't believe it, I am finally retiring!" exclaimed my friend, Elaine. "All I want to do is sleep late and read the paper from cover to cover—but I think I need to see my accountant first thing in the morning because I'm getting really nervous about my money. How do I take it out? How much should I take out? To say nothing of my really big concern, which is will my money last me? Why does it all have to be so nerve-wracking?"

Doing anything new can bring on a case of the nerves. And since retiring is a new phase of your life, it's natural to be a tad concerned. But not a nervous wreck. That's why we came up with *I'm Retiring, Now What?!* It has all you need to know, from planning your retirement budget to deciding where to live, not to mention how exactly to get Social Security and Medicare. It's both calming and smart. And there's no financial jargon, no worrisome charts and forms. Just the basics, pure and simple, and in English. You'll learn how easy it is to get a reverse mortgage or understand power of attorney. Plus, you'll get the inside track on travel for seniors (lots of neat ways to see the world) and health do's and don'ts.

So start reading. Your retirement just got a little more fun.

Barb Chintz
Editorial Director, the Now What?!™ Series

table of contents

Chapter 1 . . . the best is yet to be 6

What's it all about? **8**   Getting ready to retire **10**
Consulting and part-time work **12**   You and your partner **14**
Now what do I do? **16**

Chapter 2 your money 18

Get your finances in order **20**   Do you know how much
goes out? **22**   Income and assets **24**   What's the outlook for you? **26**
Investing during retirement **28**   How long will your nest egg last? **30**
Paying taxes during retirement **32**   Money-saving ideas **34**
Financial planners **36**   Now what do I do? **38**

Chapter 3 getting out of debt 40

Credit card debt **42**   Kicking the credit card habit **44**
Debt solutions **46**   Scams aimed at seniors **48**   Now what do I do? **50**

Chapter 4 where do you want to retire? 52

First you fantasize **54**   Keeping your existing home **56**
Reverse mortgages **58**   Selling your home **60**   Moving far afield **62**
Geographical considerations **64**   Senior Living alternatives **66**
Evaluating retirement communities **68**   Moving and taxes **70**
Now what do I do? **72**

Chapter 5 staying active 74

Indulge your hobbies and interests **76**   Start a second career **78**   Check
out volunteer work **80**   Take a trip **82**   Try traveling with a group **84**
Go back to school **86**   Now what do I do? **88**

Chapter 6 social security 90

Time to start collecting **92**   When to start taking your benefits **94**
Applying for benefits **96**   Taxes on your benefits **98**
Social Security and your family **100**   Now what do I do? **102**

Chapter 7 401(k)s and pensions 104

Your 401(k) **106**   401(k): Lump-sum distribution **108**   401(k): Leave it
with your employer **110**   401(k): Required distributions **112**   Your SEP,
SIMPLE, or Keogh **114**   Your pension **116**   Pension: Annuity payments **118**
Pension: Lump sum payment **120**   Now what do I do? **122**

Chapter 8 dealing with IRAs 124

Your accounts and taxes **126**   Individual Retirement Accounts (IRAs) **128**
IRAs: Distribution and taxes **130**   Roth IRAs **132**   Annuities **134**   Now what do I do? **136**

Chapter 9 insurance needs 138

Life insurance **140**   Medicare **142**   Medigap insurance policies **144**   Different types of
healthcare plans **146**   Health insurance—if you retire before age 65 **148**   Long-term care
insurance **150**   Buying long-term care insurance **152**   Medicaid **154**   Now what do I do? **156**

Chapter 10 estate planning 158

Your estate **160**   Wills **162**   The executor's job **164**   Power of attorney **166**   Trusts **168**
Tax consequences for your heirs **170**   Funeral planning **172**   Now what do I do? **174**

Chapter 11 longevity basics 176

Healthy living **178**   Eating right **180**   Exercise **182**   Recommended checkups **184**
Memory loss **186**   Grief **188**   Depression **190**   Now what do I do? **192**

glossary 194
index 198

...the *best* is yet to be

What's it all about? 8
A new phase of your life begins

Getting ready to retire 10
Sort out your feelings

Different ways to retire 12
"65 and out" is not the only way

You and your partner 14
Plan for more togetherness

Now what do I do? 16
Answers to common questions

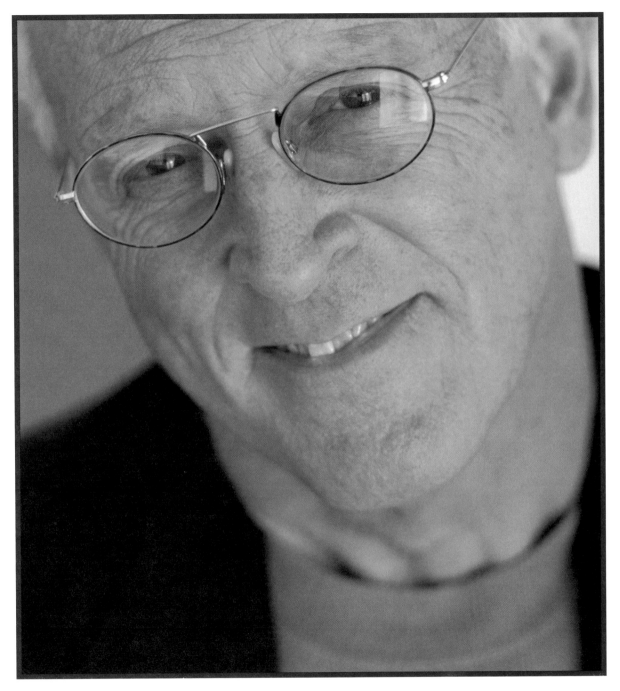

*My company is offering me
an early retirement package.
How can I tell if it's a good deal?*

what's it all *about?*

No, you are not retiring from life

YOU'RE REALLY DOING IT—you're retiring. Congratulations! You've waited for the big R all these years, and at last it's here. But what does the word retirement mean to you? Chances are, if you asked ten different people you'd get ten different answers. Some people think that retirement means, "I'll finally have the time to do all the things that I've always wanted to do." Some people celebrate with, "I won't have to get up and go to work anymore." Other people equate retirement with insecurity. "Will I have enough money to live comfortably?" Or, "What will happen if I get sick?" Or, "Will I miss having a regular schedule and a full-time career?"

Sure, retirement can be a mixed bag of emotions, dreams, and expectations, but uncertainty is normal during any period of change. Think back to other transitional points of your life. Perhaps it was your marriage, or the birth of a child. Weren't you filled with a similar anxiety, especially at the beginning? Few people get home from their honeymoon without a couple of nervous confrontations, or march home confidently from a hospital with a newborn in their arms. How do you know what to do?

Experts say these anxieties are normal when you face any transition. You can expect some highs and lows at first. The key is to take it a day at a time. Whether you made the decision to retire or it was thrust upon you, the good news is there's a lot you can do right now to ensure the years ahead are the most fulfilling of your life. So relax—you've earned it—and take a close look at your options. As the poet Robert Browning put it: "Grow old along with me! The best is yet to be."

TEN COMMON RETIREMENT MYTHS

How retirement savvy are you? Answer "agree" or "disagree" to the following questions to test your know-how. (You'll find an explanation at the bottom.)

1. I have a 401(k), and my husband has a pension. We're ready for retirement.

2. I'll spend less money in retirement because I won't have to buy lunch out every day or spend much money on clothes.

3. I love to read. That's how I plan to spend my free time.

4. If I live off just the interest from my investments, I'll be sure to have enough money.

5. My husband has a good pension. That money will provide for both of us.

6. If I work part time, I won't be able to collect Social Security.

7. I have several hobbies. I'll never be bored.

8. I don't have to worry about my investments anymore.

9. I'm going to sell my house because I can't afford to live in it on a fixed income.

10. Medicare will cover all of my health insurance needs.

Answer Key: Did you answer "disagree" to almost all of the above questions? If you did, congratulations. You have a healthy, balanced idea of what retirement is all about. If you answered "agree" to many of these statements, however, don't worry. The chapters that follow will help you get a handle on your retirement.

getting ready to *retire*

What exactly is holding you back?

FOR PEOPLE WHO ARE USED to working, retirement may be quite a shock. One day you define yourself—and your daily schedule—by the work you do. The next day you're on your own, stripped of that sense of belonging that your job may have offered.

Do you feel that you're not quite ready, mentally and emotionally, for retirement? Maybe the 65th birthday has crept up on you. Or maybe your company is easing you out the door before the traditional retirement age. Even if you don't necessarily love your job, work may still offer a sense of identity and a familiar social environment. Approach retirement with confidence by considering the following questions:

1. What exactly will you miss about your job? (Be specific.)
2. What aspects of your job won't you miss?
3. Do you feel that the work you do is important? To your company? To society? To yourself?
4. What do you envision doing in the years ahead?

Fill in the blanks below (where applicable).

At age 55, _____.
At age 60, _____.
At age 65, _____.
At age 70, _____.
At age 75, _____.

If you found it difficult to answer these questions, take a little more time to mull over the issues. Keep in mind that one of the best ways to ease the transition from a working life to a retired life is to plan ahead.

IT HELPS TO LOOK AHEAD

Leading an interesting and rewarding life in retirement will take more than financial planning. Take a minute to jot down the things you've always wanted to do—but lacked the time to pursue. Now you'll have the time. Anything is possible. So start planning.

SK THE EXPERTS

What will change in my life once I retire?

As much or as little as you want. It's all up to you. The thing to think about is what aspects of your preretirement life you want to keep. Perhaps it was the weekly paycheck that you received. If so, you might want to take a part-time job. Perhaps your routine was comforting. If so, then a slower, less structured routine might not be right for you. Sign up for regular volunteer work at a museum, your church, or your local hospital. A lot of retirees worry about how they will replace the emotional and intellectual rewards they got from work. Don't fret. The world after retirement is just as full of new and interesting challenges as it was when you were working, except now you have the time to explore!

My coworkers are my best friends. I don't think I can handle not working. What should I do?

Coworkers often provide an extended family, and work can give you a social structure that's not available in any other part of your life. You are right to be concerned about missing this. Instead of retiring full stop, you might want to downshift to fewer hours and a slower-paced schedule. That way, the work can still provide mental stimulation and social contact, but you'll no longer feel the stress of a full-time career.

I'm ten months shy of retiring, and I am already counting the minutes! How can I keep from going to pieces before my time is up?

Think about what's causing these feelings. Have your friends and your spouse already retired? Do you feel you're missing out on activities with them? Are you resentful at still being tied to a nine-to-five schedule? If that is the case, ask them to schedule some activities on weekends instead of weekdays so you can go along. You may also feel left out at the office because you are older than everyone else. If so, try to find some things in common, such as sports or movies, that you can talk about with those younger than you.

consulting and part-time *work*

RETIREES USED TO BE PEOPLE who had stopped working. But that definition is no longer accurate. More retirees work today than ever before, and many younger retirees leave their first careers early only to embark on a second, more rewarding one.

●EARLY RETIREMENT

Your company may have offered you an early retirement package. This could be great news, since many such packages contain enhanced benefits you would not have received had you retired on your own. You might get a higher pension than you've actually earned. Let's say, for instance, that you're 55 years old. Because you're taking the package, the company might credit you with five more years than you actually accrued. Your pension amount would be calculated as though you were 60 years old. Some companies may also include health insurance and other assorted perks.

Whether or not you had a choice about retiring early, finances require careful planning. Retiring early takes more money than you may think. If you retire at age 55, you've just cut 10 years off your earning power. That's 10 fewer years to put money away in a tax-deferred retirement account. You'll probably be dipping into your retirement savings for income 10 years sooner, too. That means early retirement costs you twice: on the front end, and the back end.

In addition, withdrawing money early from a 401(k) or an IRA is not always feasible. It can cost you an additional 10% in tax penalties (see page 129). The same is true of Social Security. You can collect at age 62, but you'll get less—forever—than if you wait until age 65, when you can collect full benefits.

Finding another job may be your way of dealing with the financial stress of early retirement, especially if you had no choice in the matter. If you were not given a sizable severance, work may be a necessity instead of an option. But even if you are secure financially, finding another job may also be a way of easing the transition to retirement.

● CONSULTING

Even if you are 65 and financially secure at the time you leave your job, retiring abruptly can be difficult. One day you're at work, and the next day . . . you're not. While there is no formal way to retire gradually, you can ease the separation by taking some small steps on your own.

Some retirees continue to work part time, for instance, even though they've officially retired. Such an arrangement may be for three months, or it could run indefinitely. Others retire officially but enter into a "consulting" arrangement whereby they still work at the company for two or three days each week. And still other retirees agree to work on special projects, on a freelance basis, over the next year or so.

Those are all good suggestions, you say, but not at my company. You may have to look elsewhere. Part-time, consulting, or freelance work isn't limited solely to your former employer. Consider another firm in the industry or a past client.

● SECOND CAREERS

One option, whether you retire early or not, is making a career switch. Perhaps you worked as an electrician for most of your life. After retirement, you might be interested in sharing some of your knowledge with others. Local colleges and trade schools often need retired professionals and tradesmen to teach basic courses.

Another possibility: Think about turning a hobby or interest into a small business. For instance, you may have been a Saturday painter. Now is your chance to show your portfolio to art dealers or join a cooperative gallery. Or if you were a teacher, you might want to start that children's book you've always wanted to write.

Or maybe you want to get into a new groove altogether. Take a course in designing Web sites and go for a job in that burgeoning industry. Or set up a gift shop so you and your spouse can travel around the world on buying trips. The options for second careers really are limitless.

EXPERIENCE COUNTS

Many businesses now welcome older employees. Why? They bring experience, seasoned judgment, and reliability to the workplace.

you and your *partner*

Spending more time with your spouse may take some getting used to

RETIREMENT WON'T CHANGE YOUR basic relationship with your spouse, but it may change certain aspects of it. To make sure that both your own and your partner's needs are addressed, talk together about expectations. Start by discussing what your life together has been before retirement. Use the following questions to get started:

- How much free time do you spend pursuing different interests?
- On the weekends, is it just the two of you, or are you often with other people?
- Are you happy with the current arrangement, or do you look forward to spending more free time with each other?

Talk about how you expect these and other situations in your everyday life to change when you both retire. If you don't agree, it's time to negotiate an accommodation you can both live with.

You've probably talked about the nuts and bolts of your upcoming retirement. Can we afford it if I retire now? Will we have to sell our house? How will my own routine differ? But what happens when you are retiring and your spouse is not? You may run into some complications because your life is changing—and your spouse's is not. Again, start by talking about the little things:

- Do you want to take on, trade, or hire out certain responsibilities of running the house once you've retired?
- Do you want to convert a spare room into an "office" for hobbies or part-time work?

If your spouse plans to continue working for long, you may have to come up with a temporary plan to deal with issues such as these.

ASK THE EXPERTS

My husband and I both have successful careers and are planning to retire next year. How can we prepare ourselves to make the change?

First, start talking about your expectations once you retire. You might both consider a gradual transition into retirement, perhaps by consulting or working part time. This transition lets you and your spouse practice retirement living on a part-time basis, in preparation for the day when you both leave the workforce permanently.

My wife was forced to take early retirement and is a bit depressed about it. Is there any way I can help her?

To help your wife, you must first understand what's behind her feelings. Is she upset because she feels betrayed by her former employer? Does she feel that she doesn't matter? Leaving a job, especially after many years, can be like having a death in the family. Time—and sometimes professional help—is needed to accept the loss of that way of life. But if your wife is simply feeling that she needs to be useful, talk to her about other employment options. Many early retirees go on to successful second careers.

FIRST PERSON   SUCCESS STORY

To Each His Own

Bill and I had been looking forward to our retirement for years. But on the very first morning after we retired, Bill started questioning the way I tidied up the house. "Wouldn't it make sense to start upstairs and work your way down?" he asked. "Why do you buy this brand of detergent?" Bill was barking so many orders that I couldn't believe he was the same man that I had been living with for the past 40 years. It wasn't until a week or so later that I realized he was trying to run the house—and me—much as he had run his department at work. This was not the retirement I had envisioned. I wanted to tinker around the house with no pressure. My husband needed a project to manage, but it wasn't going to be me! I found out about a group of retired executives who advise new entrepreneurs and suggested rather strongly that he sign up. He's now out of the house for a few hours every day, and I'm able to do my work in peace, and finish the crossword puzzle if I want to!

—Florence G., Princeton, New Jersey

now what do I do?

Answers to common questions

My wife is ready to retire, but I'm not. How do we resolve this issue?

Keep your job, and let your wife retire (assuming you can afford to). Don't assume that your wife needs you to be at home with her just because she's retiring. But do try to accommodate your wife's new schedule. Perhaps she wants to spend more time traveling, for example, and wants you to come along. Could you take more vacation time (unpaid, if necessary)? Similarly, if she wants you to play golf with her twice a week, consider cutting back on your working hours, if possible.

One way to combat the stress of your new situation is to draw on coping strategies that have worked for you in the past. Does reading up on a particular situation help you, for example? How about talking it over with friends, or getting an expert's advice? Do what has worked for you before in similar stressful situations.

My husband and I have just retired. Many of our friends—other couples about our age—are continuing to work part time. We think they're crazy. Are we missing something?

Not necessarily. Many working people look forward to retirement as a life of leisure. No schedules. No meetings. No alarm clocks. You finally have time to enjoy life. If this is how you feel, go with it. But keep in mind that many retirees feel that way initially. The first years of unstructured time are glorious. After that? You might begin to be restless and discover that you need some of the daily structure that work previously provided. Then you, too, might consider the possibility of working again.

My husband is planning to retire in the spring, and I'd like to retire at the same time. But every time that I think about it, I get a little anxious. I just can't imagine life without work.

For many people, work defines who they are and gives their life much of its meaning. If your work provides you with this kind of satisfaction, you may have to continue doing it, at least on a part-time basis, and make a more gradual transition into retirement.

Help! My company is offering me an early retirement package. How can I tell if it's a good deal?

If you have a choice in the matter, then consider the following:

1. How much do you stand to lose or gain financially by jumping ship early? (What will it cost you in terms of your pension, medical benefits, and/or 401(k) vested contributions? Are the incentives your company is offering worth it?)

2. What opportunities will exist on your job if you turn down the package? (Do you think that your job may eventually be eliminated and that you'll then be forced to leave without a package?)

Before you make a decision, you should probably discuss your options with a certified financial planner or an accountant (see pages 36–37). He or she can help you assess the short- and long-term value of such a package and how it fits in with your overall retirement savings plan.

OW WHERE DO I GO?!

CONTACTS	BOOKS
American Association of Retired Persons www.aarp.com	**The Retirement Sourcebook** by Mary Helen Smith and Shuford Smith
	Taking Retirement: A Beginner's Diary by Carl H. Klaus
	The Adventure of Retirement by Guild A. Fetridge
	Your Next 50 Years by Victoria F. Collins with Ginita Wall
	The Healing Journey through Retirement: Your Journey of Transition and Transformation by Hil Roth, Dorothy Madway Sampson, and Dale S. Fetherling

CHAPTER TWO

Your *money*

Get your finances in order **20**
Review what you've saved up

Do you know how much goes out? **22**
If you aren't sure, it's a good time to find out

Income and assets **24**
What assets do you have to live on?

What's the outlook for you? **26**
Compare your spending with your income

Investing during retirement **28**
Prudent investments are good inflation beaters

How long will your nest egg last? **30**
Spending down your principal

Paying taxes during retirement **32**
Uncle Sam still wants his cut

Money-saving ideas **34**
Bargains take time to find, and time is what you
have now

Financial planners **36**
What they can help you with

Now what do I do? **38**
Answers to common questions

I've been meaning to get my finances in order for years. Am I too late?

get your *finances* in order

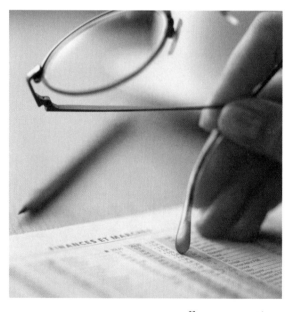

Know what you've got

YOU'VE WAITED FOR RETIREMENT for many years, and now it's here—finally! In case you're feeling a little nervous about the financial part of it, relax, it's normal. All major life transitions usually involve some sort of financial review, and retirement is no exception. Whatever you do, don't let money concerns or fears keep you from enjoying this exciting phase of life. Knowing exactly where you are with regard to your money will help answer all your questions, such as "Will my savings last as long as I do? Should I sell the house? How much travel can I afford? Should I work part time to supplement my income?"

And don't be too hard on yourself: They didn't teach retirement planning in school. So if going over your finances seems really daunting, don't fret. You can always hire a financial planner to help you get your finances in order and on the right track (see page 36 for information). But even if you do hire one, you should still have a basic understanding of your finances. So keep reading, and we'll show you what to do.

SK THE EXPERTS

I didn't start saving for retirement until after I put all my kids through college; I just assumed my pension and Social Security would be enough. Will I be okay?

Many folks put their children through college before they start saving for retirement, so they don't have a lot of years to save before they actually retire. The key to retirement lies in your spending needs: How much do you need to live on? How much do you want on hand for trips or other post-retirement activities or purchases? Even if you've never thought twice about retirement before, now it's time to have a plan.

I've been meaning to get my finances in order for years. Am I too late?

Not at all! There's plenty you can still do, even if you're already retired. During our working years, we all have good intentions about tracking our expenses or starting a budget, but few of us actually find the time. Retirement frees you up so you can finally tend to your personal finances. And it's especially important to do now, since the difference between living a full, happy retirement, and being scared to spend any money, is often having a good plan.

I've figured that my pension and Social Security check will cover my expenses. Do I still need to plan?

Yes! Inflation and taxes can have a serious impact on your retirement if you haven't factored them into your plan. Keep reading—you might uncover some issues that don't impact you today, but you might need to consider down the road.

do you know
how much
goes out?

THE BIGGEST FACTOR IN your financial plan—and the one you have the most control over—is your spending. It can be hard to measure. But the good news is that you don't need to figure it out to the exact penny; an estimate will do.

Why is it so important to start ballparking your expenses? Because when you were working, you probably had more than enough income to spend each month (even if it didn't always feel like it). With a reduced income that is often fixed, you'll have to pay attention to what goes out each month. Otherwise, you could run out of money.

There are many computer programs (like Quicken or Microsoft Money) that can help you track, as well as budget, your living expenses. If you're not up to that, simply start with good old-fashioned pencil and paper, and sketch out estimates of how much you spend each month. (See the example on the following page.) If you're not sure how much you spend in each category (most people aren't), try tracking all of your expenses for a few months in a little notebook. Once you observe your spending patterns and habits for a little while, it's easier to forecast your future expenditures.

As you estimate how much you'll need to live on when you are retired, you may find you'll spend money on entirely different things than you did while you were working (see the sidebar). Many people find that their expenses decrease by about 20% once they no longer have to go to work every day.

If you find that you have no clear idea of what you're spending, look at the sample spending sheet on the following page. It will help you track your expenses.

COMMON RETIREMENT SPENDING CHANGES

Typical increases
Health & medical

Entertainment, hobbies, travel

Telephone & utilities

Typical decreases
Clothing

Dry cleaning

Income taxes

Commuting/ parking

SAMPLE SPENDING SHEET

EXPENSE	MONTHLY	ANNUALLY
Fixed Expenses—You don't have much control over these		
Rent / Mortgage Payment		
Car Expenses: Loan Payment		
Fees & Licenses		
Insurance		
Home Expenses: Property Taxes		
Condo Dues /Fees		
Home Insurance		
Insurance: Medical & Dental		
Hospital		
Long-term Care		
Other		
TOTAL FIXED EXPENSES		
Variable Expenses—These you have some control over		
Car Expenses: Gas		
Repairs & Maintenance		
Clothing: Apparel		
Laundry & Dry Cleaning		
Alterations & Shoe Repair		
Personal Expenses: Toiletries		
Health-club Dues		
Household Costs: Decorating & Appliances		
Repairs & Maintenance		
Utilities: Gas & Electric		
Water		
Telephone/Cellular Phone/Pager		
Cable		
Computer & Internet		
Food: Groceries		
Restaurants		
Entertainment: Hobbies		
Travel		
Books, Publications, Discs		
Movies, Theater, Concerts		
Medical: Doctors		
Prescriptions		
Vision		
Dental		
Gifts and Charitable Donations		
Debt Payment		
Other		
TOTAL VARIABLE EXPENSES		
TOTAL ALL EXPENSES		

income and *assets*

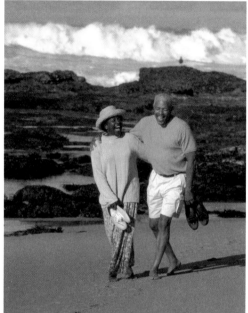

How to spend your savings

OKAY, SO NOW YOU KNOW how much money you'll need to live on. Does it seem high? Relax. Before you panic, take a deep breath and see what resources you have to cover these expenses.

The ideal way is with **income**—cash flow that doesn't require you to dip into your retirement plans or other assets. This is money that will be coming to you, be it Social Security or your pension.

Your second line of defense is income from your **assets**—your 401(k) plans (page 106), IRAs and annuities (page 128), and your other assets. If you need these assets to cover your regular living expenses, try limiting yourself to these assets' income (usually interest and dividends). For example, maybe you have a bond mutual fund that regularly pays 7% interest, which is then reinvested into the fund. Rather than selling part of the fund if you need extra money, don't reinvest the interest, but use it to live on. By leaving the **principal** (the main investment) untouched for as long as you can, you'll have it for the future.

There will come a time when you will need to go to your third line of defense—spending your assets' principal. After all, didn't you build up those assets in order to spend them during retirement? Keep in mind, however, that spending the principal can take on a life of its own—like a runaway train: the more you take out, the less income it'll provide, so the more you'll need to take out, etc. And depending on the asset, you may owe Uncle Sam capital gains tax on a portion of every sale (see page 127). If you're in a serious cash crunch, you might consider selling your home (page 60) or getting a reverse mortgage (page 58).

*t*hese are assets that you can sell to cover your living expenses. Make sure you write down the net amount—what you'd get after paying taxes, or selling fees, or paying off any debt owed on the item.

SAMPLE INCOME SHEET

FIRST AND SECOND SOURCES OF INCOME

Social Security income

Pension income

Part-time or consulting work

Annuity income

Dividend income

Interest income

Rental Income

Other Income

THIRD SOURCES OF INCOME

Savings Accounts/Money Markets

Certificates of Deposit (CDs)

Stocks

Bonds

Mutual Funds

401(k)s

IRAs

SEPs or Keoghs

Rental Property

Home/condo

Cash value life insurance

Car(s)

Art, antiques, collectibles

Jewelry, furs

Other assets

what's the outlook *for you?*

It's an ongoing process

AFTER YOU'VE PULLED TOGETHER your spending total and compared it with your monthly income, how does it look? You'll generally come to one of the conclusions below.

● Your income and/or your plan for asset withdrawal far exceed your expenses. Congratulations! Your focus should be on estate planning (page 158).

OR

● Your expenses closely match your income and/or asset withdrawal. In this case, spend some time fine-tuning your budget. First, make sure you've considered all of your regular and extraordinary expenses. Next, keep close tabs on what's coming in and going out, since inflation can gradually erode your buying power over time (see pg 28). Inflation causes your cost of living to increase, and if you're not paying attention, your expenses may eventually exceed your income. Then you might have to cut down on your living expenses.

OR

● Your expenses exceed your income and other assets. If this is the case, make your top priority cutting down on what you spend (page 40). If that doesn't bring your expenses into line, you'll want to think about your living arrangements (see page 52), since this is often the biggest expense most folks have. You may be able to change your living arrangements enough to bring down your expenses. Or perhaps you can find additional sources of income, such as part-time employment. If there is a really big gap, you might need to reconsider your decision to retire.

ⒶSK THE EXPERTS

I did a simple calculation, and things seem pretty good. Is there anything else I should do?

Good for you—all your planning paid off. That said, you need to continually review your finances. This is not a one-time exercise, it's a continuing process. Experts suggest you review your finances every month when you pay your bills. Why? Because things change. For example, inflation could suddenly rise because gas prices rose or there could be changes in the stock market, your living situation, your health. All these things and more could affect your financial stability. Try to keep on top of the changes.

My monthly income, including withdrawals from my savings, are way below my living expenses. What are my alternatives?

If the picture is bleak when you compare your income to your spending, you might want to reconsider your decision to retire at this particular time. Working a few more years might allow your assets to grow enough to make your retirement a little more comfortable. Or you may want to find a new and different job for your retirement years.

investing during retirement

Inflation eats up "safe" investments

WHEN YOU WERE SAVING for retirement, you probably followed the traditional advice: Take some risk with stocks now while your retirement is far in the future, and you'll have time to weather the market's ups and downs. Well, your retirement is here—so now what? Should you bail out of the stock market and put all of your money in a risk-free bank savings account? The answer is no, and the reason is inflation.

Inflation is that unstoppable increase in the cost of living as prices gradually go up. It's been averaging a relatively tame 3% or 4% over the past decade, so you probably didn't notice little day-to-day price increases in your milk, your clothes, or a pack of chewing gum. Applied over the years, and to bigger costs like rent, new cars, and furniture, inflation begins to add up. And the items in your budget with above-average inflation rates—health care and insurance—can really sting you.

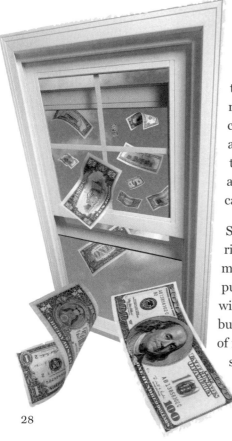

Standard retirement investment advice once was: Shift your risky stock market assets to more stable, fixed-income investments, like bonds and CDs, as soon as you retire. But if you put too much of your savings in those stable assets, inflation will erode your savings. After all, your expenses keep rising, but your assets and income stay fixed or rise less than the rate of inflation. Keeping part of your savings exposed to prudent stock market investments where you are likely to see higher returns over time can help you hold your own against inflation.

ASK THE EXPERTS

I'm not sure why I would take any money out of the stock market just because I've retired. I started investing in the market a few years ago, and it seems as though I've had high returns every year. Isn't that the norm?

Unfortunately not. Like everything else in life, the stock market ebbs and flows. Even when high returns are gushing, they inevitably slow down to a trickle—or even reverse direction for a while. That's why investment diversification is so important. Shifting part of your savings to more stable, fixed-income instruments will help protect your nest egg during the rough times while providing you with current income.

How much, exactly, should I keep in the market, and how much should I move to safer investments?

That's a great question. Deciding on your asset allocation (how much to invest in each category) is both an art and a science, and many professionals disagree over how to do it. Most financial planners calculate allocations based on your age, your risk tolerance, how much money you have, and how much money you need. Some professionals suggest an aggressive allocation of 60% stocks, 40% bonds for retirees who have a substantial nest egg. Other, more conservative planners suggest that, as a rule of thumb, retirees might match the percentage of their investment in bonds to their age. For example, if you are 65 years old, you might want about 65% of your savings in bonds; if you are 70, you might want about 70% in bonds, and so on.

how long will your *nest egg* last?

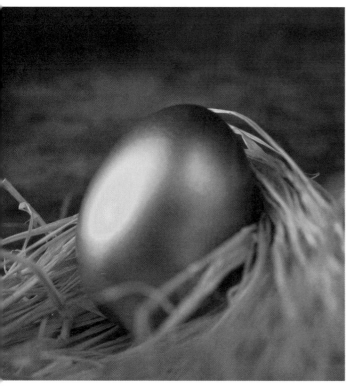

Making it last

IDEALLY, YOU WILL CONTINUE to invest during your retirement to help off-set inflation. And, with luck, the interest and dividends you earn on those investments will serve you well. But chances are, sooner or later you may want to—or have to—start dipping into those investments. This is called spending down your **principal**.

After all, you did save it to spend during retirement. But spending principal requires planning so those assets will last as long as you'll need them. According to financial planners, it's a good idea to spend no more than 4.5% of your nest egg per year.

If you want to figure out the exact amount you'll need each year and you are computer savvy, try using an electronic worksheet similar to the ones financial planners use, such as the one on the following page (furnished by T. Rowe Price free of charge on the Internet, see **www. troweprice.com**). Another one can be found at **www. quicken.com**.

Retirement Planning Worksheet

This worksheet gives you a quick estimate of the total amount of money you're likely to need for retirement. The final amount shown is based on the percentage of your current income you will need in retirement. This estimate does not take into account any income you may derive from Social Security or your employer's pension plan. That means the amount shown in this estimate may be overstated if you expect significant income from these sources.

If your current assets will not be sufficient to fund your retirement, this worksheet will show you the amount you must save, each and every year, to reach your designated asset total. It's assumed that all of the money will be invested in tax-deferred accounts, such as an IRA or 401(k) plan.

BUILD   **ANALYZE**

1 Enter your CURRENT SALARY (example: $30,000) — $ [   ]

2 Enter your TAX RATE (example: 27%) — 27% ▲▼

3 Enter the estimated INFLATION RATE (example: 4%) — 4% ▲▼

4 Enter the number of YEARS until your retirement (example: 30) — [   ]

5 Enter the number of YEARS you expect to live in retirement (example: 20) — [   ]

6 Enter the PERCENT OF SALARY you need after retirement. A general rule of thumb is that you will need between 60% and 80% of your preretirement income to maintain your lifestyle (example: 70%) — 70 %

7 Enter the RATE OF RETURN you expect to earn on your retirement savings after you retire. You might earn a lower rate of return after retirement, reflecting a more conservative investment strategy. You may wish to review historical returns for different investment categories (example: 7%) — 7% ▲▼

8 Enter any CURRENT INVESTMENTS in **taxable** accounts. Give a total number that includes your savings accounts, mutual funds, etc. (example: $20,000) — $ [   ]

9 Enter the RATE OF RETURN you expect to earn on your current **taxable** investments between now and retirement. You may wish to consult historical returns (example: 9%) — 9% ▲▼

10 Enter your CURRENT ASSETS in **tax-deferred** accounts, including IRAs, 401(k)s, etc. (example: $50,000) — $ [   ]

11 Enter your expected RATE OF RETURN on tax-deferred accounts before retirement, based on historical returns, if you wish (example: 9%) — 9% ▲▼

[ANALYZE]   [RESET FORM]

This worksheet provides only an estimate based on the information you provide.

Back to Top

31

paying taxes during
retirement

How to pay Uncle Sam after you retire

JUST BECAUSE YOU'LL NO LONGER have withholding taxes taken out of a paycheck doesn't mean you won't owe taxes once you retire. What's more, Uncle Sam wants his tax money right away. You have two choices about how to pay. You can either make **estimated quarterly payments**—taxes you pay and send to the IRS every three months—or have your taxes **voluntarily withheld** from your monthly Social Security check, pension, and regular distributions from your IRA. If you don't do either of these, you will be hit with penalties when you file your annual return. (For Social Security withholding, simply file form W-4V or W-4P for pensions and 401(k)s and annuities. For your IRA, ask your broker for the proper form to fill out for voluntary withholding taxes.)

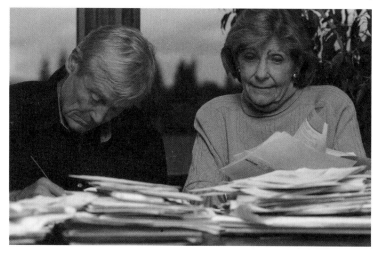

If you stop working (or cut down substantially), your income will no doubt be less. The good news is, you'll drop into a lower income tax bracket. That lower bracket can mean you owe less in taxes when you sell stock or withdraw money from retirement accounts. But some other investment strategies might change as a result. For example:

● You might want to pay off your mortgage, since your tax advantage on the interest may no longer be as attractive.
● Tax-exempt bonds (and their lower yields) are probably no longer a good investment choice for you. Consider looking for higher-yielding investments.

TAX CHANGES AND BREAKS THAT FAVOR SENIORS

HOME SALES A one-time profit of up to $500,000 ($250,000 if you're single) is not taxed if you meet certain requirements.

SOCIAL SECURITY Benefits are only partially taxable (see page 98).

STANDARD DEDUCTION The standard deduction increases for people 65 and older.

LIFE INSURANCE BENEFITS & INHERITANCES Proceeds from these windfalls are generally not taxed.

VETERANS' BENEFITS These are not subject to income tax.

PUBLIC ASSISTANCE Most financial aid for the elderly, such as winter energy subsidies, Nutrition Program for the Elderly, and other welfare programs, are not taxable.

CREDIT FOR THE ELDERLY If you're over 65 and your gross income is less than $17,500 ($25,000 if you're married filing jointly and you both qualify; $20,000 if one of you qualifies), you might be eligible for a tax credit of up to $1,125.

STATE INCOME TAXES Many states give additional tax exemptions to seniors. Some states also exclude retirement income like Social Security, pensions, and IRA withdrawals, from taxation.

WHICH IRS PUBLICATIONS DO YOU NEED?

You can order IRS Publications by calling 800-TAX-FORM or download them from **www.irs.gov**.

Paying Quarterly Taxes	No. 505	Pension and Annuity Income	No. 575
Older Americans' Tax Guide	No. 554	Medical and Dental Expenses	No. 502
Social Security	No. 915		

REVISITING MEDICAL EXPENSES

Now's the time to take a look at medical bills. You can deduct medical expenses exceeding 7.5% of your income. Some expenses that qualify (see IRS Publication 502 for more):

Doctor fees
Hospital costs
Prescription drugs
Eyeglasses and contacts

Dental costs (including false teeth)
Certain long-term care insurance premiums (see page 152)
Medical insurance premiums, including Medicare Part B (see page 142)
Hearing aids
Crutches

Wheelchairs
Transportation to and from medical providers
Certain medically-related retirement home costs
Health-related improvements to your home such as constructing wheelchair ramps, widening doorways, installing grab bars and railings or modifying stairs

money-saving *ideas*

Bargains take time to find— and time is what you have now

ARE YOU COST-CONSCIOUS? It's probably a habit you've meant to develop for years. But since your income may be decreasing now, it's a good time to start thinking about how you can cut costs. This is especially true if you have debts you're trying to pay off: The sooner you eliminate the interest that piles up each month, the sooner you can more fully enjoy your retirement. (See page 40.)

Start with senior discounts. At 65, and sometimes as early as age 55, you can qualify for discounts on airfare, trains, hotels, car rentals, movies, and restaurants, just by asking. But you do have to ask, wherever you go (and be ready to show ID indicating your age). Most reservationists or cashiers won't give senior discounts without your prompting them. For even more senior spending clout, consider joining AARP, formerly known as the American Association of Retired Persons (see below). They provide members over the age of 50 and their spouses a plethora of information about bargains and discount services.

AARP (American Association of Retired Persons)

For only $10 a year, anyone over 50 can join. For more information, visit their Web site at **www.aarp.org**, call 800-424-3410, or e-mail member@aarp.org. You can also write them at: AARP, 601 E St. NW, Washington, DC 20049.

RED FLAG

Fewer working hours mean more hours available to Spend! Spend! Spend! Don't get caught in the spare-time spending trap, or you'll lose a hunk of money before your retirement really gets going.

COST-CUTTING IDEAS

- Transfer credit card balances to low-rate no-annual-fee cards. See **www.bankrate.com** or **www.bestrate.com** for a list of low-cost cards. Pay your balance in full every month to avoid interest.

- Learn to say no to friends and relatives who ask for money.

- Comparison shop—you'll save money on your purchase *and* reduce impulse buys.

- Take advantage of free services and activities offered by local libraries and parks.

- Trade in your health-club membership and join the local YMCA or YMHA. These organizations also offer low-cost programs and activities, many geared toward seniors.

- Stay accountable: You and your spouse can encourage each other to keep spending habits in check. If you're single, find another senior friend who'd like a money-buddy and meet at least once a month to share spending victories and struggles.

- Review your insurance coverage (see Chapter 9). When you retire, dropping or reducing life and disability insurance can make sense. Don't buy insurance (or a warranty extension) for anything you can afford to replace.

- If you need a car, consider buying used instead of new, especially if it's certified and still has some warranty protection.

- Always shop with a list to reduce unnecessary purchases.

FIRST PERSON   SUCCESS STORY

Time Is Money

I admit it. I retired without having enough money to keep up my lifestyle. Because I could no longer afford to shop till I dropped, my cleaning lady had to go and I started doing the housework myself. I got pretty fast at it, and the house looked better than it had in years. Still short of money, I decided to quit buying takeout. I dragged out my old cookbooks and began to enjoy fixing my meals, like when I was young. I was soon giving friends treats from my kitchen in lieu of gifts, and inviting people over for lunch instead of meeting them at restaurants. For family birthdays, I gave IOUs promising to chase down comparative prices, or baby-sit, or mend or repair things, or do other time-consuming chores and errands. Instead of giving money to charities, I started volunteering, and met a number of interesting people. Now my money goes a lot further, I'm never bored, and I've got a bunch of new pals, too.

—**Tina P., Louisville, Kentucky**

financial *planners*

Get professional money help

WHEN YOU HAVE TO MAKE an important health decision, you enlist a doctor. If you need legal help, you call a lawyer. So when it comes to making big money decisions, don't be afraid to contact a certified **financial planner**.

What exactly will a financial planner do for you? If it's your first visit, the planner may ask what prompted your visit. If you want to address an emergency (debt consolidation or handling your company stock options), the planner will help you with that problem. If you ask for a complete fiscal examination, the planner may ask to see your tax returns, investment statements, and other financial documents to help get an overview of your situation. The planner should ask about your goals. Then the planner will recommend some of the best ways to get you where you want to go. This might mean helping you with a budget, or suggesting changes in your investment scheme, or helping you calculate the amount of insurance you need.

FEE ARRANGEMENTS

HOURLY You pay the planner for time spent meeting with you and researching your situation. This is the best place to start if you don't know exactly what you want. Fees range from $75 to $200 per hour.

PERCENTAGE OF ASSETS If you hire an investment adviser to manage your money, the annual fee is usually a percentage of the dollar value of assets managed (usually .75% to 1.25%). This is the best option if you have $100,000 or more to manage and want ongoing help.

COMMISSION Most brokerage houses and insurance companies offer free retirement planning services to their customers. If you then use a stockbroker or life insurance agent to purchase retirement assets, you pay a commission on anything you buy.

ASK THE EXPERTS

Where can I find help in locating a financial planner?

The Garrett Planning Network is a national group of financial advisers committed to providing independent, objective financial advice to average consumers. All of their advisers work on a fee-only basis and charge anywhere from $100 to $150 per hour. Contact them at 866-260-8400 or visit **www.garrettplanningnetwork.com**.

The National Association of Personal Financial Advisors is a national organization with strict membership requirements for admittance. They provide referrals to fee-only planners; call 888-FEE-ONLY or visit their Web site at **www.napfa.org**.

The Financial Planning Association is a national organization of planners. Their Consumer Service and Planner Search (800-282-PLAN or **www.fpanet.org /plannersearch/index.cfm**) provides information about choosing planners and allows you to select planners by zip code.

WHO CAN HELP

The following professionals have passed a licensing exam (or series of tests) in their specialty. They must also complete continuing education to keep their license:

Name (Abbreviation)	Area(s) of Expertise
Certified Financial Planner (CFP)	A wide range of financial areas, including taxes, investments, and insurance.
Certified Public Accountant (CPA)	Taxes and accounting.
Certified Financial Analyst (CFA)	In-depth knowledge of investments.
Chartered Life Underwriter (CLU)	Life insurance.

now what do I do?

Answers to common questions

I've tried to budget in the past, but I get overwhelmed pretty easily when I try to figure out what I spend. Any tips?

Start small. Tracking your expenses can indeed be overwhelming. But don't panic. You're not going to be able to track and project every single cup of coffee you buy or newspaper you purchase. But don't let that keep you from trying. First, start collecting receipts from every purchase you make. While you might have to work up the courage to sort through them, you'll need these receipts in order to remember what you've spent. (Some folks prefer to keep a little notebook and then write down everything as they go.) And as you write checks, make sure to write down the date, check number, payee, amount, and description of each. Then once or twice a month, sit down with your receipts and your check register and credit card statements to track what you've spent. If you're PC literate, consider compiling these in personal finance software (like Quicken). If you want to do it by hand, create a blank form like the one on page 23, and make several photocopies. As you pull together the amount you spent in each category for the week, month, or whatever period you decide to track, put the numbers in the appropriate column. Within 4-6 months you'll probably have enough history to come up with an estimate of what you spend in a year!

My home is full of furniture and crafts I've gathered over the years. Now I want to move to a smaller home. Is there any way to get some extra money for this accumulation of stuff?

First, drop by several antique stores in the neighborhood and talk to the buyers about the items you want to sell. If they think your furnishings sound promising, they may come by and give you an evaluation. (Furniture from the 1950s and 1960s is highly valued by knowledgeable buyers at present.) For items that don't make it as prized heirlooms, consider a yard sale—but only if you have an enterprising spirit, for yard-sale aficionados love to bargain. If you can't haggle with the best of them, put your goods in the hands of a company that runs estate sales, and they will auction your items for you. They'll charge a fee based on a percentage of the sales, but they will take all the hassle out of the experience for you.

Now WHERE DO I GO?!

WEB ADDRESSES

www.quicken.com/retirement/
www.smartmoney.com/retirement/
These sites provide a variety of financial
information about retirement planning.

www.seniors.gov
This government site links you to a
plethora of retirement resources.

www.investoreducation.org
This Web site provides a wide variety of
resources, including investing basics,
help choosing an adviser, and basic information about online investing.

www.invest-faq.com
This site features a collection of frequently
asked questions about investments and
personal finance, including stocks, bonds,
discount brokers, information sources,
retirement plans, etc.

www.aaii.org
This American Association of Individual
Investors site has information on stocks,
bonds, and portfolio management.

www.ftc.gov
The Federal Trade Commission's site
provides text of consumer publications
for consumer credit, investments, and
telemarketing.

www.pueblo.gsa.gov
This government site provides a wide
variety of helpful consumer publications.

BOOKS

Last Minute Retirement Planning
By Stephen M. Rosenberg, CFP

You've Earned It, Don't Lose It
By Suze Orman

**Ernst & Young's Retirement
Planning Guide**

getting out of *debt*

Credit card debt **42**
Has credit card debt always been a problem?

Kicking the credit card habit **44**
It's not as hard as you think

Debt solutions **46**
There are ways out

Scams aimed at seniors **48**
High debt can make you gullible for a get-rich-quick scam

Now what do I do? **50**
Answers to common questions

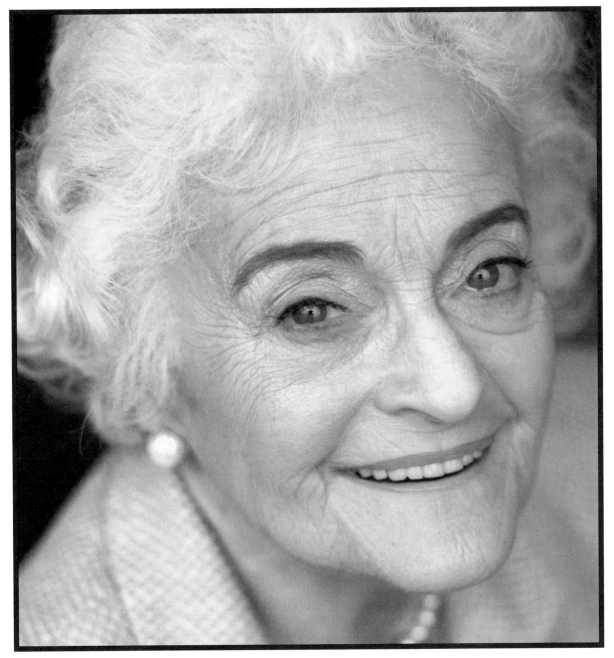

"My spouse passed away several years ago, and I'm having trouble living on a fixed income. How can I lower some of my bills?"

credit card *debt*

*Avoid high
interest debt*

IF YOU ARE LIKE MANY PEOPLE, when you see something you like in a store, you plunk down your credit card and take it home. Then you pay what you can and let the debt pile up. When you were working, it wasn't so bad—chances are, you even paid a few bills outright. But now that you're retiring, paying ever mounting credit card bills on a fixed income can quickly become hazardous to your financial health.

What's the problem here? It's called **interest**. As you know, whenever you borrow money, you need to pay for the cost of borrowing it. Why? Because if lenders weren't lending it to you, they could be investing it and earning interest on the investment. You are now their investment, so you have to pay them interest. Banks charge the **prime interest rate** for lending money to their most credit-worthy customers, usually 7% to 10%. When you sign up for a credit card, however, they can charge any interest rate they want, usually from 9% to 20%. They call this their **annual percentage rate**, or APR.

And then there's one more tiny problem: it's called **compound interest**. This means that interest will be applied not only to your initial purchase but also to any successive interest you owe. In other words, you will pay interest on interest. Say you buy a large-screen television for $1,000 and charge it on a credit card with an APR of 18%. If you just pay the minimum balance of, say $10.00 for a year and then pay it off, guess how much you really paid for the television? A whopping $1,183.00. Compound interest is a bit like yeast in that it feeds on itself. That's why you don't want to carry credit card debt.

ASK THE EXPERTS

How can I find a cheaper credit card?

Online financial Web sites make it easy to find competitive interest rates. Two sites that compile a comprehensive range of card deals are **www.bankrate.com** and **www.bestrate.com**.

How can I switch my balance to a cheaper card?

After finding the best deal, first tell your current cardholder about it and ask them to match it. Often they will, because they don't want to lose your business. If not, inform the company you are switching to, and they'll explain how to transfer the balance.

What happens if I don't pay my minimum payment?

Not a good idea. As far as the credit card company is concerned, that minimum payment is a loan payment. If you miss the deadline, they report it to the various credit bureaus that keep track of your credit rating, and it is recorded on your credit report as a missed payment. This can hurt your credit rating.

60 SECOND SAVINGS

If you make larger purchases just after the monthly closing date for your credit card, you can get a free loan for almost two months. The closing date is the last day that your purchases were recorded for that month's bill. It is usually printed on the bill near the credit and cash advance limits and current balance.

For example: Your card's closing date is August 24, and on August 25 you buy your girlfriend a $150 necklace and earring set for her birthday. When your next bill is issued on about September 3, the charges made after August 24 won't appear on it, so the jewelry charge won't be there. You don't owe anything until the following bill is mailed on October 3. Then you would ideally pay the entire balance by the end of your grace period (usually after 25 days or so).

Compare that with what happens if you pay a small amount every month for a whole year. At the typical credit card interest rate of 17%, you pay $175 for the same jewelry.

kicking the credit card *habit*

Avoiding the perils of living on credit

LIVING ON A FIXED INCOME can be a shock to many new retirees, especially if their monthly income is lower than what they are used to having. Using credit cards to bridge the gap becomes all too tempting, especially when new credit card offers keep arriving in the mail. Within a year, many new retirees are looking at whopping credit card bills with interest as high as 20%. They can't afford to pay it off and they can't afford not to!

Help is at hand. You can extricate yourself from your debt mess. The first thing to do is quit denying that you have a credit problem.

WHAT IF I CAN'T CHANGE BY MYSELF?

If you have trouble breaking the bad-debt syndrome, consider joining Debtors Anonymous, a national not-for-profit collective where you'll find others working to beat the same problem. There are no dues or fees.
P.O. Box 920888
Needham, MA 02492
Tel: 781-453-2743
www.debtorsanonymous.org
e-mail: **new@**
debtorsanonymous.org

STEP BY STEP:

CUTTING BACK

1. SHIFT YOUR DEBTS TO THE LOWEST-INTEREST CREDIT CARD YOU CAN FIND. You can put debt from other cards onto a new card. This makes sense if you get a low interest-rate card.

2. LIMIT YOURSELF TO ONE CARD. You don't need more than that. Avoid store cards; they're usually the worst deals of all. The 10% to 20% discount some offer you to sign up is quickly canceled out by the higher interest rates you pay on your purchases.

3. CANCEL ALL OTHER CARDS. You don't want to leave unused credit cards open. Avoid the temptation: Snip the cards and send the issuer a letter informing them you are canceling.

4. THINK OF CREDIT CARDS AS EMERGENCY CASH. Cards can be invaluable in covering a health emergency or necessary car repair. They should be used as backup when your ordinary budget plans go awry— not as mad money that stretches your buying power.

5. DRAW UP A SPENDING BUDGET. Making your expenses fit preset limits is a very effective way to keep debt, especially credit card debt, in check.

debt
solutions

You don't have to find a way out all by yourself

IF YOU HAVE HAD TROUBLE with high debt, whatever you do, don't go to one of those "debt doctors" who advertise on a telephone pole or on late-night TV. Private companies often charge high fees, and the field is full of charlatans who prey on desperate people. Also avoid private bill-paying services, especially those that claim they can fix up a poor credit record.

There is, however, reasonable, low-cost help to be had. A credit counselor working for a public or not-for-profit agency is the best way to go. For a small fee, the agency typically contacts all of your creditors, negotiates a moratorium on payments to them, and sets up a plan to repay them. But bear in mind that you will be put on a tight leash until it's over; these payments will be made on a fairly aggressive schedule. Your creditors get much of your incoming cash, while you are allowed to keep only an allowance for your essential living expenses.

If this seems frightening, ask the counselor for help in drawing up a budget. If the budget looks totally impossible, he or she can arrange a more lenient payment schedule.

ASK THE EXPERTS

Can debt consolidators really fix my bad credit rating?

The answer is no. They may claim they can magically clean up a bad credit report, but that is not true. Only you can clean it up, and it's not by using magic. You have to contact each creditor and work out a payment plan. Some may agree to lower your interest rate for this purpose. Once your debts have been paid, you can ask your creditors to report your clean slate to the credit bureaus so your credit history shows your improved status.

How long will it take me to get out of debt?

The answer is usually the same amount of time you have been in debt. In other words, if you have been struggling with too much debt for three years, that's about how long it will take to get clear of it.

Where can I find a credit counselor?

The National Foundation for Consumer Credit is the nation's biggest group of not-for-profit credit counselors. They can direct you to a local office. Consumer Credit Counseling Services, Tel: 800-547-5005

FIRST PERSON   DISASTER STORY

Over My Head

My husband had his own business and made a good living, but wasn't a great saver. When he died at age 60, there was no retirement nest egg, just some stock that I went through pretty quickly to pay the bills. Social Security didn't come close to what he made. I guess I didn't want to see this, so I just charged things as usual. Before I knew it, I was $30,000 in debt. I got so upset I landed in the hospital with high blood pressure. My kids found out about the debts and paid them, and that made my blood pressure really soar! I had to do something. I got rid of all my credit cards and am learning to live a new way: cash and carry. It was tough at first, but I'm managing. Instead of giving the kids and grandkids things, I give them my time—funny thing, they like that better.

—Miriam S., New York, New York

scams
aimed at seniors

How can you outsmart them?

YOU'VE MADE IT THIS FAR without falling prey to swindlers' tricks. Why should you worry now? No matter how sophisticated and educated newly retired folks are, they're prime targets for smooth-talking con artists. An experienced crook knows just how to play on financial fear and insecurity.

While you don't want to become paranoid, it's important to look at how you make decisions. Big-ticket items like vacation homes, insurance, and investments require careful thought, analysis, and discussion—not sales pressure. Even if someone approaches you with a deal that sounds interesting and legitimate, never buy on the first meeting. Instead, gather printed information and say that you'll call back when you have had a chance to look it over. Then analyze the offer.

Let's say someone gives you an intriguing sales pitch for a surefire investment. Ask yourself:

● Do you know anything about the investment? Are they using a lot of technical language to sway you with their expertise? Does the salesman immediately begin pressuring you to sign something? Do you personally know any of the salesperson's clients?

● Are the terms too good to be true, for example, a guaranteed 20% return on your investment in the first year? Don't let your need for money blind you to deals that are full of smoke.

● If you decide to go along with the investment, is there any waiting period within which you can back out of the deal? If you change your mind, can you get your money back in full? If the answer is yes, can you get that in writing?

SIGNS OF A SCAM

● **ANYTHING FREE:** TV sets, dinners, or vacations. Remember the old saying: "There's no such thing as a free lunch." If it's free now, you'll no doubt pay for it down the road.

● **A SQUEEZE TO SIGN.** If it's "now or never" and you don't have the option to review the papers with your spouse or adviser before you sign, it's probably a scam.

● **TOO GOOD TO BE TRUE.** If it sounds like that, it probably is—especially "ground floor opportunities" from anyone other than intimate friends or family members. Even loved ones can draw you into an ill-advised investment without meaning to.

● **RECOVERY ROOMS.** Services that help you recover money you've lost from past scams—for a fee—are usually also scams.

● **"CHURNING" FOR FEES.** If a broker frequently suggests buying and selling securities, you might be paying unnecessary commissions.

● **DOOR-TO-DOOR CALLERS.** Few legitimate outfits sell door-to-door these days, and building inspectors, home contractors, and other "professionals" who show up unannounced are rarely on the up-and-up.

● **GET RICH QUICK.** Most newspaper, TV, or radio ads that "guarantee" your ability to get rich quick are really veiled attempts at getting your money from you quicker.

● **MIRACLE CURES.** Direct mail or other pitches that sell cures for aches, pains, and diseases are rarely aboveboard. Stick with your doctor for medical advice.

● **YOU'RE A BIG WINNER.** Letters claiming you only have to return the card to be a big winner are selling something. Read the fine print and see what you're buying—book, magazine, or something else—and make sure you want it. Your chances of winning a prize are less than they would be in the lottery.

CONSUMER WATCHDOGS

Securities and Exchange Commission (SEC)
Protects consumers from investment fraud. Contact them at 800-SEC-0330 with questions or complaints about investment offerings or investment advisers. They also provide free publications, like "Questions You Should Ask About Your Investments."

Federal Trade Commission (FTC)
Polices everything from fair credit to telemarketers to food labeling to identity theft. Contact their Consumer Response Center (877-FTC-HELP; 202-326-3128 or at **www.ftc.gov**) with complaints or to request free consumer education pamphlets.

Better Business Bureaus
These agencies help consumers fight unfair or deceptive business practices in your area. Check your local phone book for contact information.

now what do I do?

Answers to common questions

If my credit card debt is so bad, how come companies keep offering me more credit cards?

Credit card companies have more liberal lending guidelines than banks or other credit institutions. Credit card companies calculate that you can carry debt equal to 36% of your annual gross income, while debt counselors suggest 20%. Credit card companies want you to run up bills because they make their profits from all that interest you're paying. So the more you spend, the more often your mailbox seems to fill up with offers for yet more credit cards from companies eager to take advantage of your penchant for spending.

Which debt should I pay first?

Pay down the most expensive debts first—those with the biggest balances at the highest interest rates, since they're costing you the most. Work your way down to the smallest, lowest-interest debts.

What if a creditor is harassing me?

That is against the law. Bill collectors are not allowed to use threats, advertise your debt to the public, or phone you repeatedly about it. If one does, contact the Federal Trade Commission (FTC). It monitors and investigates complaints about consumer credit practices.

Federal Trade Commission
600 Pennsylvania Ave., NW
Washington, DC 20580
Tel: 877-382-4357
www.consumer.gov or www.ftc.gov

I have a huge credit card debt at 19%. What can I do?

Review all your retirement savings accounts. Use some of that money to pay off your high-interest debt. Then see if you can raise cash by selling or borrowing against any assets, such as a house or car. If you own your home, you can apply for an equity loan using your house as collateral (an asset of yours that the bank can make claim to if you default on the loan). You may also want to consider getting a **reverse mortgage** to help pay down the debt (see page 58). You can also apply for a **personal** or **consolidation loan**. Here a bank agrees to loan you a lump sum of money which you use to pay off your credit card debt. Then you immediately begin paying back the loan, but at a much lower interest rate. If you have no assets, you may need someone who does to co-sign the loan for you.

NOW WHERE DO I GO?!

WEB ADDRESSES

www.loanweb.com
www.bankrate.com

PUBLICATIONS

The Money Diet
by Ginger Applegate

Guide to Understanding Personal Finance
by Kenneth Morris and Alan Siegel

Your Money or Your Life
by Joe Dominguez and Vicki Robin

CHAPTER FOUR

Where do you want to *retire?*

First you fantasize **54**
And then do your homework

Keeping your existing home **56**
There are both pros and cons

Reverse mortgages **58**
Here's a way to pay for your living expenses

Selling your home **60**
It can open the door to new adventures

Moving far afield **62**
Consider less conventional possibilities

Geographical considerations **64**
Many locations offer advantages for retirees

Senior living alternatives **66**
The services can make this a real retirement

Evaluating retirement communities **68**
It pays to look carefully

Moving and taxes **70**
State income tax is not the only consideration

Now what do I do? **72**
Answers to common questions

I'm itching to move to another part of the country. How can I be sure it'll work out before I make the leap?

first you *fantasize*

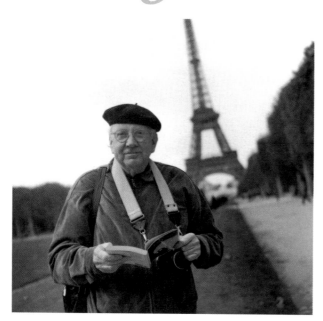

Chances are, you'll live in more than one place during retirement

DECIDING WHERE TO LIVE when you retire can be a bit overwhelming. But don't get discouraged. There are lots of resources to get you started. Here's what you need to consider:

YOUR LIFESTYLE: What do you want to do during your retirement? Baby-sit for the grandkids? Improve your golf handicap? Train for the marathon? Grow tomatoes? Raise money for your favorite charities? Take up scuba diving? Travel as much as possible? Is where you are living now conducive to your retired lifestyle? Or will the weather or location hamper your plans?

YOUR FINANCES: After you retire, how much money will you need to stay where you are? (See page 56.) Can you afford to stay? If you are just getting by, do you want to rent out a room to help defray the cost? Or is it smarter for you to sell and move to a rental?

YOUR HEALTH: This is tricky, but try to imagine your well-being in the next 5 or 10 years. For instance, if you have a bum knee now, it's likely that climbing stairs will prove increasingly difficult in the years to come. In that case, selling your two-story house sooner rather than later might be a good idea.

FACTS TO CONSIDER

Do you have a fantasy about where you want to retire? Maybe you want a tropical beach, or a handy golf course, or a water view. Or you might want to live in another country altogether. Once you identify your dream location, look at how it might measure up in the long run:

- Would your everyday lifestyle fit in your dream location?
- Is the place close enough to friends and family (or far enough away, if you want to keep them at a distance)?
- How's the climate? Is the terrain easy to navigate? Do you notice a lot of seniors walking around?
- Is public transportation accessible? You might reach a point when you or your spouse can no longer drive.
- How available is quality healthcare?
- Is it easy to do weekly grocery shopping and run errands? If you like restaurants and nice shops, are there some nearby?
- Is the neighborhood a low-crime area?
- How available are events and activities you like: concerts, plays, sports events, museum or library visits, educational opportunities, etc.?
- Are there any activities or services designed just for seniors?
- What about the cost of living and the taxes?

EVALUATING LOCATIONS

Retirement Places Rated: The Single Best Source for Planning the Retirement You Deserve by David Savageau provides an in-depth discussion of many variables for retirement living, and uses them to evaluate 187 cities across the country. The top ten in the 5th edition are:

1. Fort Collins/Loveland, Colorado
2. Charleston Sea Islands, South Carolina
3. Henderson/Boulder City, Nevada
4. Wickenburg, Arizona
5. St. George/Zion, Utah
6. Boca Raton, Florida
7. Scottsdale, Arizona
8. Tucson, Arizona
9. Prescott/Prescott Valley, Arizona
10. Fort Myers/Cape Coral, Florida

keeping your existing *home*

MANY PEOPLE WANT TO REMAIN in the comfortable familiarity of their own home when they retire. They enjoy living near family and friends, being part of their community, and staying in the place they've called home for many years. Before you decide to stay put, evaluate some options:

YOUR LIFESTYLE: Will staying suit your lifestyle? If your retirement vision is a daily nature hike, but your home is in the middle of a big city, you might want to seek out other possible living arrangements.

There's no place like it

YOUR FINANCES: Can you afford to stay put? If your mortgage payment has traditionally consumed most of your paycheck, how will you cover the monthly expenses with your retirement income? It might be wise to try to pay off the mortgage before retiring; check with your financial adviser to find out whether or not selling investments to do that would be advantageous in your particular situation. If your mortgage is paid off, your adviser may suggest getting a **reverse mortgage** (see page 58) to give you some money to live on.

YOUR HEALTH: How will your changing physical needs impact where you live? If you drive everywhere now, you might find your location burdensome if and when you can no longer use your car—unless there's good public transportation nearby.

ASK THE EXPERTS

We've always wanted to stay in our home, but now the kids are all married. We're wondering if our house is too big for us. What should we do?

Don't just hang on to your home out of inertia; you're likely to become overwhelmed and let it fall into disrepair. When the house isn't a family hub anymore, and you're ready to spend time on other things, it's time to think about moving on.

I'm itching to move to another part of the country. How can I be sure it'll work out before I make the leap?

Take a test drive before you make a commitment and sell your home. There are several organizations available to help you swap your home with people in other parts of the country. They can help you arrange for a short-term or long-term house swap. Contact HomeLink U.S.A. at 800-638-3841; **www.homelink.org** or HomeExchange at 805-898-9660; **www.homeexchange.com**.

I'm in serious debt. How can I tap the equity in my house?

If you're moving to a smaller home, you can pay off debt with some of the profits from the sale of your old house. If you're staying put, you can apply for a home equity loan or a second mortgage. If you are spending your savings to pay off the debt, a reverse mortgage (page 58) might replace income lost from those savings.

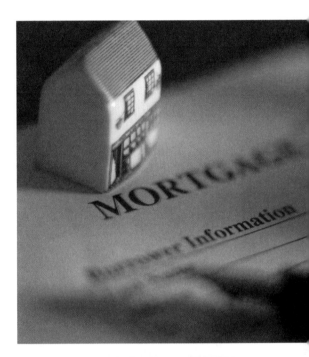

PAYING OFF THE MORTGAGE

Many people find that paying off their mortgage by the time they retire is advantageous, both financially and psychologically. But it isn't always a good idea to tap assets to pay off your debt. It comes down to crunching the numbers. Compare the interest rate your investment earns with the interest rate your loan charges. Which is higher? In most cases, it makes sense to take cash from an asset that earns a low rate of interest to pay a debt with a high rate of interest. But assets earning a high rate of interest usually shouldn't be spent to pay a debt with low interest.

reverse
mortgages

Get money to stay put

IF YOU WANT TO STAY where you are, but you aren't sure you can afford it, a **reverse mortgage** might be your ticket to homestead bliss. You're a good candidate if your house is mostly paid for, you're at least 62 years old, you've maintained your home in good condition, and you plan to live there indefinitely.

In a reverse mortgage, you "sell" the bank your house, but you get to live there for as long as you live. In return, the bank makes a payment (or series of payments) to you, usually for 60% of your home's appraised value. Unlike other loans that you need to repay right away, a reverse mortgage isn't repaid until after your house is actually sold, which typically doesn't happen until it's sold by your heirs. (If the heirs want to keep it, they'd have to repay the loan.)

There are three basic types of reverse mortgages:
TENURE REVERSE MORTGAGE—You receive fixed monthly payments for the rest of your life.
TERM REVERSE MORTGAGE—You receive monthly payments for a fixed number of years. The payments are usually higher than those for tenure types.
LINE OF CREDIT REVERSE MORTGAGE—You receive a specified line of credit that you may draw on. Only the amount you use, plus interest, is deducted from the eventual sale price of the house.

You can also get a combination of these methods, or even a lump-sum amount up front. But if you want a lump sum, compare terms of any reverse mortgage offer with regular mortgages, since regular mortgages are often cheaper.

Before you're approved for a reverse mortgage, for your protection, you're required to talk with an independent HUD certified credit counselor (no charge). If you have questions about the application procedure, contact HUD at 800-569-4287 for a referral, or visit their Web site at **www.hudhcc.org**. The AARP's Home Equity Information Center (202-434-6042; **www.aarp.org**) can also help.

ⒶSK THE EXPERTS

How much money can I get from a reverse mortgage?

This varies depending on your age, the lender you use, your home's value, the loan costs and interest rates, and the type of loan you choose. If you own your home free and clear, you should get about 60% of its worth.

Will a reverse mortgage impact my Social Security benefits?

No—the money you get from the bank is technically a loan, so it does not impact your taxable income, and therefore it will not affect your Social Security. (Remember, it's the amount of money you declare as income on your taxes that impacts your Social Security payment.) However, the proceeds may impact your participation in income-based programs such as Medicaid or food stamps.

How do I shop for a reverse mortgage?

You want to do an apples-to-apples comparison, since the costs associated with a reverse mortgage can vary widely, and may be very high (possibly up to 10 percent of the loan value). Ask each potential lender to give you a **standard cost disclosure**, also known as a total annual loan cost or TALC. This is a standardized form that banks will give out about their loans to help consumers compare reverse mortgages. Typical costs that show up on this statement include closing costs, insurance, an origination fee, and a monthly servicing fee.

EXPERIENCE COUNTS

For more about reverse mortgages, contact:

Fannie Mae
800-732-6643; **www.fanniemae.com** and request a publication titled *Home Keeper: It Pays to Keep You in Your Home*

Federal Trade Commission
202-326-2222; **www.ftc.org** and request *Facts for Consumers: Reverse Mortgages*

National Center for Home Equity Conversion
7373 147th St. West, #115, Apple Valley, MN 55124; **www. reverse.org** to compare costs of different reverse mortgages

National Reverse Mortgage Lenders Association
202-939-1760 or **www. reversemortgage.org** for a list of lenders who provide reverse mortgages.

SAMPLES OF REVERSE MORTGAGE MONTHLY PAYMENTS
Based on a home worth $225,000, and an 8% interest rate

Your Age	Mortgage Sum	10 Years of Term Payments	Lifetime of Tenure payments
68	$ 85,295	$1,050	$ 642
75	106,899	1,316	854
85	141,108	1,737	1,379

selling your *home*

Make a fresh start

WHAT IF YOU WANT TO SELL? Though moving can be stressful, a fresh start may be just the right thing. If your home is too much to care for, or if keeping it would stretch your budget too far out of line, or if you're looking for a change of venue, leaving for greener pastures can be the answer.

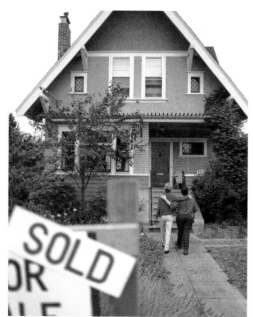

Financially speaking, you could be looking at quite a windfall. Let's say your $300,000 house is fully paid for, but living there would cost $300 a month in property taxes, plus maintenance and cleaning costs of another $200 a month. Then assume that you sell it and invest the proceeds of $280,000 (after closing costs) at, say, 6%. You would get $1,400 a month; plus the $500 you'd save by not having to pay property taxes and the ongoing maintenance costs. If you think you could find and enjoy a home or apartment that would cost considerably less than this, then selling your house might be a very sound idea.

Letting go of your house can be a big relief. It might be nice living in a more compact home in a location that is better suited to retirement (think no stairs, easy upkeep, nearby public transportation, sunny climate, etc.).

O.K., there is, of course, the chore of moving, especially if you have to sift through stuff you've accumulated over the years. But look at it this way: You can dispose of your keepsakes exactly as you want. If you stay put and suffer some health setbacks, all that sorting out will be left to your children or other family members. If you do the job now, you could save them the trouble later on.

ASK THE EXPERTS

Unloading our empty nest sounds like a good idea. But where would we go?

You have many options. If you simply want a smaller place, consider checking out condominiums, especially those catering to seniors. Or maybe take the leap and move to another part of the country (see page 62). If you're tired of home owner-ship, try renting. Look into retirement communities. It's true, some are very expensive, but others are rea-sonable. Senior living facilities have good security, safety devices, activities, cleaning services, and often meals and other amenities. Start looking early— many of the best ones have waiting lists.

I'm recently widowed. I'd like to stay at home, but I don't want to live alone. Any suggestions?

Finding a roommate can help, whether you're looking for companionship or simply want to reduce your expenses. The National Shared Housing Resource Center (www.nationalsharedhousing.org, 770-395-2625) coordinates over 300 homesharing programs across the country. They can help whether you're looking to rent a room from some-one else, or would like to open up your home to another individ-ual. They also provide careful screening and background checks.

TAX CONSEQUENCES OF SELLING A HOME

The current tax law says that you can sell a home without paying the usual capital gains tax on the first $500,000 in profit ($250,000 if you are single). You must have lived in the house for at least two of the past five years before the sale.

moving far *afield*

Looking for something out of the ordinary?

AS THE POPULATION CONTINUES TO AGE, new retirees are finding or creating living arrangements to fit their lifestyles. Here are some more options that might strike your fancy:

RESORT COMMUNITIES These luxurious retirement communities provide the amenities of resort living: golf, tennis, swimming pool, beaches, marinas, scenic views, exercise rooms, and a variety of dining facilities.

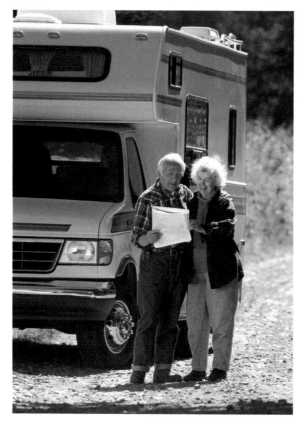

Most have resort prices to match. Call 630-871-3303 or see **www.retirementresorts.com** for more information.

FOREIGN COUNTRIES Some folks long to live out their fantasy of retiring to some tropical island paradise. It's important to investigate how living abroad affects Social Security, voting, visas, income taxes, etc. For example, retirees living abroad aren't eligible for Medicare. Check with American Citizens Abroad (1051 N. George Mason Drive, Arlington, Virginia 22205, fax: 703-527-3269, **www.aca.ch**) or Transitions Abroad (800-293-9373, **www.transitionsabroad.com**) for more information.

RV LIVING Why not go mobile? Some folks can't wait to sell everything they have, buy a motor home, and take that tour of the country they've always dreamed about. See **www.rvamerica.com** or call 480-784-4771 for more information.

ASK THE EXPERTS

I'm thinking about renting a little rustic villa near the Gulf of Mexico for a year to try it out while I rent out my house in Connecticut. What do I need to consider?

It's a great idea to live in your potential retirement location for a test period. It's important, though, to understand the tax consequences before you start. During the time that you rent out your place, you'll have to file a Schedule E with your tax return to report any income you earn from the rental. Of course, you'll get to deduct any related expenses, like advertising, repairs and maintenance, insurance, and any costs of managing the property from afar. You might also be able to deduct any return trips you make to Connecticut during the year, if you can show that the reason for the trip was to manage your rental property. If you decide to move permanently, you'll be able to sell your house with little or no tax consequences as long as you meet the IRS requirements (see pages 32–33). If you continue renting out your home indefinitely, plan on paying tax on the gain.

I'm intrigued by the concept of shared housing, but I'm concerned about living with a stranger. Any tips?

The best shared living arrangements happen when the people involved understand their individual needs and desires and can communicate them to each other. Consider your motivation for the arrangement. Are you simply looking to trim costs? Or do you just want another person in the house to check on you in case you fall or get sick? Or are you looking for a potential companion with whom you can go shopping, take walks, and attend the theater? As long as you and your potential roommate are in sync, sharing a home can be a mutually beneficial experience.

geographical *considerations*

Seeking greener (or warmer) pastures

IF YOU'RE SET ON PULLING UP STAKES, where will you go? Maybe a city where you have friends or relatives sounds appealing. Perhaps year-round sunshine and warmth is calling. Maybe you're yearning for a mountain view. Regardless of your motives, it's important to thoroughly check out your prospective surroundings before you actually pick up and go.

How should you start? There are enough "Top 50 Places to Retire" lists to keep you busy investigating for the next few years. But don't let them confuse you. There's really no such thing as the perfect place to retire. After all, everyone's preferences are different—it's a matter of knowing what's important to you. But you can enjoy the process of learning about new cities, investigating your alternatives, and doing your homework.

The process of picking a spot might seem intimidating at first. It's like choosing a marriage partner—sometimes you just know. But like any thoughtful courtship, you need to be patient and get to know your potential mate. Don't rush into anything right away. Consider visiting your possible destination town at least four times (once during each season) before you make a long-term commitment.

BACK TO COLLEGE

College towns are popular choices for seniors because they offer a nice cross between big city culture and small town friendliness. Many colleges and universities offer lifetime learning opportunities that can help seniors stay active. A good example is the North Carolina Center for Creative Retirement (NCCCR), which is part of the University of North Carolina at Asheville. An integral part of the university, the NCCCR provides local seniors opportunities for education, leadership, and community service.

WHERE SHOULD I START?

These sources advise on the best places to retire.

Money Magazine (www.money.com/money/depts /retirement/bpretire)

Modern Maturity, May-June 2000 issue

about.com (seniorhousing.about.com)

Retirement Places Rated, a book by David Savageau containing information about more than 180 cities, along with their weather, crime statistics, activities, medical services, and more.

America's 100 Best Places to Retire, by Richard L. Fox.

FIRST PERSON   SUCCESS STORY

Retiring Right

When I retired, I wanted to just lounge around the house. My wife, Marsha, wanted to move to a retirement community, but I persuaded her that we'd be better off staying in our own place. After all, the mortgage was paid off, and I was still fit, so I could take care of the maintenance. The kids did come over every Sunday for dinner, and Marsha had always liked cooking for them. But soon I realized that although I had retired, she was still doing the same work she had always done—cleaning the house, doing the laundry, running the errands, fixing the meals. I was having fun, but she had no more free time than she'd had before. Then my eyesight began to go, and we finally had to move to a retirement community. It has housekeeping services, two meals served every day, and a van to take us to stores and doctors' appointments. There are lots of activities for us to enjoy here. And now the kids have us over to their house for Sunday dinner. Marsha loves it. I wish we'd moved earlier, so Marsha could have retired when I did.

—**Martin L., Phoenix, Arizona**

senior living *alternatives*

Can you get along on your own, or do you need assistance?

THERE ARE SEVERAL STYLES OF GROUP accommodations, sometimes referred to as "congregate living." Here's an overview of what they include.

INDEPENDENT LIVING Also called retirement communities, these are geared toward seniors who want to remain independent but who may want the convenience of meals, housekeeping, some shared activities, and transportation to shops and doctors if needed. Many communities have a nurse on duty, and may allow people to use electric carts to get around the halls or paths. Often transportation is available to take residents to markets, shops, and doctors, and special outings may be planned as well. If you go this route, you're on your own to pay for it—no insurance or federal assistance will help.

ASSISTED LIVING These units provide the same wide range of services as independent-living facilities, plus personal and medical care for people who are not as robust physically as they once were. Services range from simple medication reminders to help with **activities of daily living** (ADL), such as shopping, bathing, grooming, and dressing, as needed, in addition to many services independent-living facilities might offer. Long-term care insurance (see page 152), and possibly Medicaid (see page 154) may help defray assisted living costs.

NURSING HOMES These long-term care (or skilled nursing) facilities provide 24-hour support for people with chronic and long-term illnesses, who need more than limited assistance. They generally provide a full range of services, including daily nursing care, and dietary and therapeutic assistance. Medicaid and long-term care insurance can help defray these costs, and Medicare may chip in for short-term stays.

CONTINUING CARE RETIREMENT COMMUNITIES (CCRCS) These communities combine all three types of living arrangements mentioned above in adjacent facilities. They allow retirees to graduate as needed from independent-living quarters to assisted-living quarters and then to a nursing home—all in one location (usually a campus setting). Residents "age in place" without having to move every time their situation changes. Such facilities are especially convenient for couples; if one requires nursing care, the other lives close enough to visit easily.

ⒶSK THE EXPERTS

How much does it cost to live in a retirement community with continuing care?

The facilities can be vastly different, and so can the prices. Some communities are made up of a cluster of cottages or a renovated apartment building, while others consist of luxurious houses and town houses grouped in a country-club setting. Although a few continuing-care communities provide rental arrangements, an up-front payment is usually required (anywhere from about $30,000 for a studio apartment to several hundred thousand dollars for a detached home) in addition to ongoing monthly fees. The up-front payment may be nonrefundable or only partially refundable to your heirs when you die. The monthly fees increase as you move from one level of care to the next.

I've heard there's a lot of paperwork involved when you move into a congregate-living facility. Can I get stung?

It's a good idea to have an elder-care attorney, an accountant, or another senior specialist review the contracts and fee structures of all congregate-care facilities before you sign up, to help you evaluate all the costs. The payments and fees for continuing-care residences, assisted-living facilities, nursing homes, Medicare (page 142), Medigap insurance, and any long-term care insurance you have (page 152) can all impact your income taxes. Even the initial or monthly fees for a living facility may be considered medical expenses and might be partially deductible. But if you move away, part of any up-front payment you make could be forfeited. Also, if you don't have unlimited funds, you will want to find out if the assisted-living and nursing-care facilities you are considering accept Medicaid, and when and how you might be eligible for it.

evaluating retirement communities

A RETIREMENT COMMUNITY IS USUALLY an independent-living facility, often with continuing-care amenities, such as medical assistance or help with activities of daily living. Choose a retirement community very carefully. Before you visit one, call for a brochure and compare the information in it with this checklist. If questions remain unanswered, ask them by phone. Based on what you find out, you will be able to decide which facilities you will actually visit.

Call first, then visit

✔ Do units have private, full bathrooms? Step-in showers?

✔ Do units have cooking capabilities?

✔ Do units have individually controlled heating and cooling?

✔ How extensive are housekeeping services?

✔ What security procedures are in effect in the building?

✔ What types of religious services are available?

✔ Are there guest accommodations?

✔ Is there a beauty/barber shop?

✔ Is there access for the handicapped?

✔ Are there several meal plans? Can special dietary needs be met?

✔ What types of social activities are provided?

✔ What types of medical, rehabilitative, and therapeutic services are available?

✔ What are the costs and fees?

✔ Which services cost extra?

✔ If there is a nursing facility, does it accept Medicaid? Medicare?

EVALUATING A RETIREMENT COMMUNITY

When you narrow down your options based on location, costs, and services, make appointments for thorough tours of your top choices. Here are points to cover:

✔ Talk to the administrator. Does he or she answer questions readily? Ask to see the facility's license and the administrator's license. Are they up-to-date? Review the facility's inspection reports. Are there any issues or problems noted? If so, have they been resolved?

✔ Talk to the staff. Are they pleasant? Patient? Do they seem easily available to residents and guests? Are there enough of them?

✔ Is the living unit you are considering convenient to the dining room? Is there ample closet and storage space? Are there emergency call buttons or pull cords in the room? Grab bars in the bathroom? Is there enough privacy?

✔ Investigate the medical services. What happens in case of emergencies?

✔ Is the lighting bright enough in the common areas? Are there handrails in the hallways? Room for electric carts in the hall? Wheelchair accessibility? Elevators?

✔ Are there fire sprinklers? Smoke detectors? How secure are the residents' units? The facility itself?

✔ Are the public rooms and activity rooms neat? Attractive? Are the lawns and gardens well kept? If there's a pool, is it clean?

✔ Eat a meal. How's the quality and taste of the food? Look at the weekly menus. Is there enough variety? Are the menus nutritious? Are the kitchen and dining areas clean and inviting?

✔ Talk to the residents. Ask them what they like about the place. Ask what they don't like. Do their interests seem to be similar to yours?

moving and *taxes*

Cost of living, taxes, and other dollar signs

SOME PEOPLE MOVE TO A DIFFERENT state just to save on income taxes. While saving money is always fun, especially if you are on a fixed income, don't make hasty decisions just because a state doesn't have an income tax. Here's why:

● Low state income taxes, or even none, doesn't mean total tax relief. For example, Florida doesn't have a state income tax. They do, however, have an "intangibles tax" that taxes nonretirement plan savings. Since most retirees have high accumulated savings, but not huge incomes, this tax structure can actually be a liability rather than a benefit. You should also consider real estate taxes, sales taxes, and whether Social Security and pension benefits are taxed. Remember— every state gets money to conduct its business somehow.

● Because your income may be lower during retirement, taxes probably won't be as burdensome as before. When you were in the 28%, 31%, 36% or 39.6% federal income tax bracket, every dollar of deductions counted, and every additional dollar of income got taxed heavily. But many retirees find themselves in the lowest 10% federal income tax bracket, so their overall tax burden is more manageable. Even the tax rate in a high income tax state like California is less than 10%. When combined with a 15% federal income tax, the total percentage is still less than you probably paid during your high-earning years.

● Taxes are just one component of the total cost of living—the price of housing, utilities, food, clothing, etc.—which is the real issue to take into account. Consider Arkansas, for example. The state income tax rate ranges up to a hefty 7%, but the overall cost of living is lower than in most other states.

STATE TAXES AT A GLANCE

Add the following information into the mix of ingredients you're considering as you ponder moving. But if you find yourself putting a lot of weight on these factors, make sure to visit your accountant before making any final decisions.

TAX ADVANTAGES

States with no income tax

Alaska

Florida

Nevada

New Hampshire

South Dakota

Tennessee

Texas

Washington

Wyoming

States with no sales tax

Alaska

Delaware

Montana

New Hampshire

Oregon

TAX DISADVANTAGES

States that tax Social Security benefits

Colorado

Connecticut

Iowa

Kansas

Minnesota

Missouri

Montana

Nebraska

New Mexico

North Dakota

Utah

Rhode Island

West Virginia

Vermont

Wisconsin

States with no real estate tax breaks for seniors

Florida

Louisiana

Minnesota

Oregon

Vermont

Wisconsin

now what do I do?

Answers to common questions

I've found a beautiful retirement community, but I don't know if I will really like living there. How can I make up my mind?

Almost all of these communities have guest rooms with very reasonable rates. Move into one for a week or two and take part in all the activities. If you like the residents and enjoy many of the activities, it's a good bet you will enjoy living there. And the guest-room rent for the week is a small price to pay compared to the cost of moving if you find out later that you don't like it.

What expenses for assisted living or nursing care will be covered by long-term care insurance, Medicare, or Medicaid?

Medicare usually only pays for a short period of care following a hospitalization (see page 142). Depending on your policy, long-term care insurance not only pays a per diem if you go into a nursing home, it also pays for an aide as soon as you need assistance with two or three activities of daily living (or ADLs). ADLs include eating, dressing, bathing, using the toilet, and transferring in and out of beds and chairs. Assistance with ADLs is not limited to congregate-care facilities; you can get help in your own home as well. You will get similar payments from Medicaid, provided you have no other source of income.

I've heard that refinancing my existing mortgage is a good idea. Should I do it?

If your motivation to refinance is pulling out cash from your home, you may want to compare the costs of refinancing with a reverse mortgage (see page 58). It might also make sense to refinance if you have at least 10 years or so remaining on your current mortgage and could reduce your rate by at least 1.5% to 2%—provided you plan on living in the house for many years to come.

I'm feeling a little overwhelmed at the prospect of selling my home that I've lived in for the past 40 years. Who can I turn to for help with the real estate market?

Consider calling a Senior Real Estate Specialist. These specially trained real estate agents have completed certain courses and other prerequisites geared toward helping older individuals find homes that meet their needs. You can locate one at www.seniorsrealestate.com, or call 888-822-7423.

OW WHERE DO I GO?!

WEB ADDRESSES

American Association of Homes and Services for the Aging
www.aahsa.org
National nonprofit organization representing 5,600 not-for-profit nursing homes, continuing-care communities, assisted-living residences, and community service organizations for the elderly. (AAHSA, 2519 Connecticut Avenue NW, Washington, DC 20008-1520, Tel: 202-783-2242, Fax: 202-783-2255).

www.50states.com
Provides a variety of information about all 50 states, including fun facts, virtual tours, weather, and real estate (50 States, Box 2216980, Santa Clarita, CA 91322).

www.homemods.org
National Resource Center on Supportive Housing and Home Modification, 3715 McClintock Avenue, Los Angeles, CA 90089-0191, Tel: 203-740-1364, Fax: 213-740-7069.

BOOKS

Retirement Places Rated
By David Savageau

AARP: "Housing" and "Selecting Retirement Housing" pamphlets
800-424-3410

Money magazine annual issue on "Best Places to Live"

America's Best Places to Retire
By Richard L. Fox

Fifty Fabulous Places to Retire in America
By Kenneth A. Stern and Lee Rosenberg

Home Planning for Your Later Years: New Designs, Living Options, Smart Decisions, How to Finance It
By William K. Wasch

CHAPTER FIVE

Staying *active*

Indulge your hobbies and interests 76
What's your secret desire?

Start a second career 78
If you'd still like to work

Check out volunteer work 80
If getting involved is one of your main objectives

Take a trip 82
You can stay more than a week now

Try traveling with a group 84
They take care of the details and offer new companions

Go back to school 86
Pursue the college major you couldn't take before

Now what do I do? 88
Answers to common questions

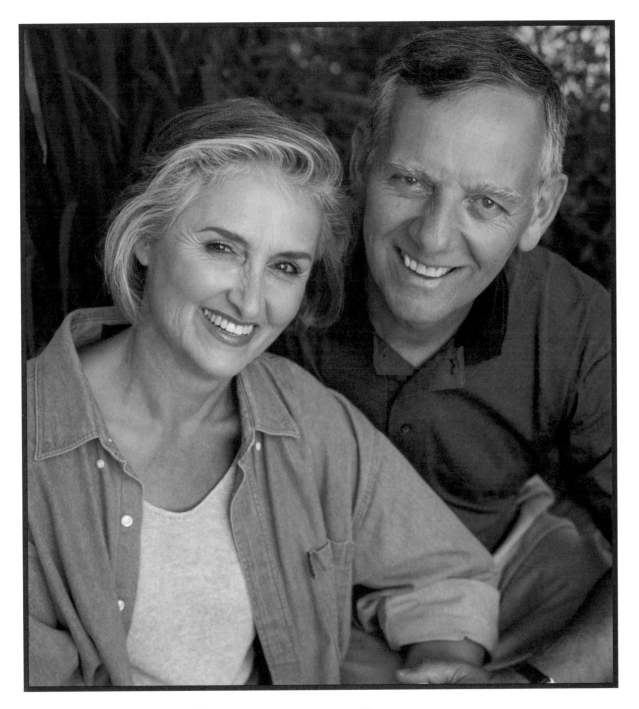

We love to travel. How can we find other retirees who share our travel interests?

indulge your *hobbies* and interests

Time to do what you want

PEOPLE ARE RIGHT IN THINKING that retirement is the time to do all the things they've been putting off—acting in community theater, golfing every day, cooking French food, growing prize roses, painting portraits, or reading Homer's *Odyssey*—in Greek. If you're an avid photographer, for example, you can now pursue your hobby full throttle and enter photography contests, take courses, join clubs, and spend as much time taking pictures as you like.

But what if you spent so much time working that you didn't get a chance to develop many outside interests? Or if you've lost interest in the hobby you thought you'd pursue once you retired? Take heart. A healthy retirement is about change and growth. The trick is to find interests that intrigue you. Here are some considerations for finding a new hobby you'll enjoy:

● **Do you enjoy being alone, or do you prefer a group?** All hobbies have certain events that bring enthusiasts together, but for some hobbies, such as playing bridge, you need a group, whereas other hobbies, such as writing poems, require periods of solitude.

● **Be realistic about your talent, your patience—and your expectations.** If you're just learning to knit, will you get discouraged trying to make that intricately patterned mohair coat? Start with a simple scarf.

● **How much do you need to spend to get started?** It's wise to keep initial costs low until you're sure you really enjoy a particular hobby. Rent—rather than buy—a violin, for instance, during the first few months of lessons.

- **Consider the space limitations in your home.** If you move to smaller living quarters, will you have enough space for a table saw?
- **Talk over your plans with your spouse.** Do you expect him or her to join you for golf or not? How much time do you imagine spending on it? Will your spouse resent your being gone that long?

COMMUNITY GROUPS

If it's a structured activity that you seek, community centers and senior clubs offer many such events for retirees. Membership fees are low (or free), and you can get involved as much, or as little, as you wish. This is an ideal way to make new friends who share common interests. Churches and synagogues run programs, too, that offer lunches, study groups, and bus trips to nearby points of interest. Often the programs are nonsectarian; that is, you may not have to be Catholic to attend a church's bingo night or join their string ensemble. Civic groups run clubs for retirees, as well. The Rotary Club, for example, sponsors Probus clubs for retired men and women who are active volunteers. They sponsor social events and schedule speakers to keep members informed about local issues.

FIRST PERSON   SUCCESS STORY

A Priceless Legacy

After I retired, I had free time to spend with my grandchildren, and I began to tell them stories about my own childhood. They love to hear about the "olden days." One day my daughter, their mom, overheard me telling the kids how we used to shear sheep on the farm. She said she'd never heard it, and asked me to write it down for her, because after me there would be no one who knew about the way things were back then. Soon I started writing a page or two every day—nothing complicated, just how things were different when I was young—the first telephone we had, the first tractor we owned, how my dad fought in World War II. Soon after that I took a course in writing family history at the local community college, and my cousin and I gathered up all the old family pictures we could find and labeled them with names and dates as best we could discover them. I've continued to write about the good old days, and now I've started compiling our genealogy. At all the family gatherings, everyone crowds around to hear what I've found. They all love what I'm doing for the family. I love it, too.

—Lee F., Billings, Montana

start a second *career*

Strike out in new directions

MANY RETIREES STAY with the job they know—they are rehired as consultants by their old firm. They can often set their own hours while keeping a more independent stance. That way their situation may be less pressured than their old job was (see opposite page).

Other retirees want to work, even need to work, but not at the same old job. They want to go on to new careers. If you are ready to explore a change but think you're not qualified to do anything but sell software, for example, or balance the books, you may be shortchanging yourself. With a lifetime of experience from your paid employment—and from your volunteer activities, interests, and various home and social roles, too—you have more skills than you may realize. Can your write reports and memos? Supervise others? Gather information? Organize records? Lead a group? While you may have used any or all of those skills at your old job, they are certainly not limited to one particular occupation or profession. Other, completely different jobs may require similar skills.

If you're thinking about changing careers, take some concrete steps:

- Assess your skills by listing them on a piece of paper.
- Network with friends and business associates to get their opinion about how good a fit you'd be in the new field. Ask them for job leads and/or introductions to others in the profession.
- Find out if you'll need formal training for the job you have in mind.
- Consider volunteering in the desired field to gain some experience and to make some connections.

SAME JOB. . .DIFFERENT HOURS

I loved my job, but hated the daily stress and grind. How can I keep my hand in?

Lots of people retire "officially," yet they continue to work in their old professions—but at a reduced level. Some retirees cut back to two or three days per week, for example. Others work just a few hours every day. Such arrangements need to be worked out in advance with your boss and/or the human resources department before you retire. In some cases, your part-time stint can run indefinitely; in other cases, it's for a limited time only. The deal you cut will depend on your employer, your relationship with the company, and the type of work that you do.

A lot of retirees I know consult or work freelance. Some get paid by the project, some by the hour. Which is better?

In the final analysis, it comes down to your time. If you know how many hours are involved in a project, then you can calculate a project fee. If you don't know how a project will pan out, consider charging by the hour to make sure you get paid for any unforeseen "overtime." A note of caution: When you work on a project basis, you're often called in when deadlines are bearing down on regular employees. You may find those deadlines affect you as well. After 12 straight hours at your desk trying to help your colleagues out of a jam, you may well wonder if this is the way you want to spend your retirement.

START YOUR OWN BUSINESS

At some point in our lives, we've all dreamed of owning our own business. But for most of us, it has remained just that: a dream. Being an entrepreneur is risky—and time consuming. (You generally need to pump a lot of money into a fledgling business, too.) Still, running your own business can be rewarding, and lots of retirees have done it successfully.

Do you have what it takes to succeed? Consider the following questions before you take action:

- What kind of business do I want? (Can my hobby become a business?)
- How much money is needed to start the business? How much money will I need to keep it going?
- Am I prepared to work really hard?
- Do I have a business plan?
- How will I get started? What resources do I have?
- Do I have someone I can ask for guidance during the start-up?

check out *volunteer* work

Keep using your experience and skills

YOU WANT AN ACTIVE, meaningful life after retirement without taking a job? Volunteering can fill the bill. Nearly 50% of all people aged 55 and older volunteer at least one day a year. Many people log far more volunteer days than that, of course—and in a surprising number of occupations. These giving souls work not just as aides in hospitals and schools, but as tutors and foster grandparents, proofreaders and programmers, nature guides, and special-events coordinators.

Volunteering lets you "give back" to a community. For many folks, that can be enormously rewarding. In fact, it can improve your life in a concrete way. Research has proved that regular volunteering prolongs life expectancy and improves physical and psychological well-being. Why? When you volunteer, you tend to feel better about yourself and the world around you. You also may feel less isolated, less absorbed with your own problems and worries.

Doing good, though, isn't the only reason to volunteer. It can give you the opportunity to meet new and interesting people who share your passion for, let's say, saving endangered animals. For many retirees, volunteer work also provides structure and routine—a natural extension of your working life. You can continue to use skills and talents you've developed over the years—but in new and interesting ways.

FINDING VOLUNTEER WORK THAT'S RIGHT FOR YOU?

The AARP (American Association of Retired Persons) suggests using the following questions as a guide:

1. Why do I want to do volunteer work?

2. What are the benefits I expect to derive from my volunteer service?

3. What particular knowledge, skills, or aptitudes do I have to offer?

4. What are my strengths?

5. What do I like doing? What do I dislike doing?

6. Do I enjoy working alone or with others?

7. Is there something I want to learn how to do?

8. Is there a particular problem or issue that I care about? What really interests me?

9. Would I rather work with people, things, or ideas?

10. Am I willing to travel?

11. How much time am I willing and able to give?

12. Are weekends or weekdays best? What part of the day—morning, afternoon, or evening—would suit me best?

WHAT'S OUT THERE?

- Points of Light Foundation (800-865-8683) connects you with local volunteer opportunities through its national network of volunteer centers.

- Habitat for Humanity International (800-422-4828; www.habitat.org) builds homes for needy families, both here and abroad.

- The Special Olympics (800-700-8585; www.specialolympics.org) provides sports training and athletic competition for children and adults with mental retardation.

- Marine Toys for Tots Foundation (www.toysfortots.org) collects, wraps, and distributes toys for kids during the holiday season.

- The Susan G. Komen Breast Cancer Foundation (800-653-5355; www.raceforthecure.com) sponsors the Race for the Cure.

- The Virtual Volunteering Project (www.serviceleader.org/vv) provides information on more than 100 organizations across the U.S. that use online volunteers to do research, tutor students, and translate languages (among many other jobs).

take a *trip*

Now's the time to get up and go

MOST PEOPLE TALK ABOUT TRAVELING as they do about losing those last five pounds: I'll do it someday. Well, guess what? That someday may be here at last. In retirement, you're no longer constrained by work or family commitments. You have the time to travel. Your biggest problem, in fact, may be picking a destination.

If there's a culture you've always wanted to know more about, a cuisine you adore, or a style of architecture you want to study, that's a good starting point for picking the place you want to visit. In which towns, cities, or countries can you pursue those interests?

Next, think about how long you want to stay at a particular destination. Then consider your budget. That may not be as tough as it once was. As a senior, you can take advantage of money-saving senior discounts, such as the following:

● Join the AARP and save up to 25% on airfare, hotels, motels, resorts, car rentals, and cruises. (To join, you must be over 50; there's a $10 annual membership fee.)

● Almost all airlines give special discounts to travelers over 62 on virtually all their flights. Just tell the reservation clerk your age when you book your itinerary. They also sell books of coupons that can be used by seniors for trips at reduced prices.

Finally, decide if you want to travel alone, with a spouse or partner, with friends, or as part of a group. And before you pooh-pooh the group option, keep in mind that times have changed. Senior group travel doesn't necessarily mean a bus trip that shuttles you from one sight to another anymore. (See page 84.) Today, the over-50 crowd demands more challenging adventures, both physically and intellectually. You can take a tour to hike, paint, cook, study, or even learn a language with other like-minded retirees.

VOLUNTEER AND SEE THE WORLD

Commitments vary from a week to a few months. Some volunteer travel programs pay for your travel expenses, but if you pay, they may be tax-deductible.

- Elderhostel Service Programs (877-426-8056, **www.elderhostel.org**) Go to far-off places—some foreign— where you build homes, teach children, catalog artifacts.

- Global Volunteers (800-487-1074; **www.globalvolunteers. org**) Help handicapped children in Ecuador, for example, or teach English in Southern Italy.

- Earthwatch Institute (800-776-0188; **www.earthwatch.org**) Work with scientists and conservationists on field research projects in 50 countries.

- The International Executive Service Corps (203-967-6000; **www. iesc.org**) Business and professional types become consultants in developing countries.

- Health Volunteers Overseas (202-296-0928; **www.hvousa. org**) Nurses, physical therapists, doctors, and other health professionals go to work in developing countries.

try traveling with a *group*

Travel with retirees who share your interests

VIEW PINK DOLPHINS. Improve your Spanish. Hike in the Himalayas. Or take an African safari with your grandchild. These aren't your father's "old folks" tours. Rather, they're educational, cultural, historical, and athletic adventures that will inspire and enrich your life. You'll meet new friends, learn new things, and yes, visit new places. The main advantage of a tour is that most everything—booking, baggage handling, driving, and obtaining tour guides—is done for you.

Typically, you have to be at least 50 years of age to sign up for treks designed for retirees, but if your spouse or traveling partner is younger, he or she will be allowed to go with you. Here's a sampling of what these senior groups have to offer:

ELDERHOSTEL (877-426-8056; **www.elderhostel.org**) provides educational adventures throughout the world. You can pan for gold in the Yukon, for example, or get an insider's view of the Metropolitan Museum. Their catalogs include some 2,000 different educational and cultural trips. Inspired by the youth hostels of Europe, Elderhostel offers low rates: A six-night stay for a U.S. trip, for example, costs about $500 plus round-trip transportation.

SENIOR WORLD TOURS (888-355-1686; **www.seniorworldtours.com**) offers snowmobiling adventures in Yellowstone National Park and in Alaska. Trips run for 6 to 10 days.

GRAND TRAVEL (800-247-7651; **www.grandtrvl.com**) organizes cultural and educational vacations for grandparents—and their grandchildren (ages 7 to 17), in the U.S., Europe, Africa, and Australia. Groups are limited to 20 people. The most popular trip: the two-week African safari in Kenya.

SENIOR WOMEN'S TRAVEL (212-838-4740; **www.poshnosh.com**) specializes in cultural tours "for women only" to Paris, Venice, London, and more. The group also offers a grandmother/granddaughter trip to Paris.

ELDERTREKS (800-741-7956; **www.eldertreks.com**) offers adventure travel to remote destinations such as Iceland, Transylvania, Tibet, and the Galapagos Islands. Groups are small (just 16 people). All trips involve walking; some also include hiking in the rain forest, for example, or sailing (with a small crew) off the coast of British Columbia.

EUROPEAN WALKING TOURS (217-398-0058; **www.walkingtours.com**) lets you "walk" through Italy, Austria, Switzerland, Spain, or France. No backpacking is involved, though. You're based in a hotel and spend your days exploring the region on foot. The trip to the Dordogne area of France, for instance, lets you explore the prehistoric caves.

WALKING THE WORLD (800-340-9255; **www.walkingtheworld.com**) tours some 27 destinations in the U.S. and around the world. By day you'll walk the countryside; by night, you'll sleep in a bed-and-breakfast or a country inn. Groups are limited to 16.

ODYSSEYS UNLIMITED (888-370-6765; **www.odysseys-unlimited.com**) offers fully-escorted cultural and sightseeing tours to China, Spain, and other countries outside North America. Groups are relatively small (no more than 24 people per group).

OVER THE HILL GANG, INTERNATIONAL (719-389-0022; **www.othgi.com**) sets up skiing, rafting, biking, and golfing adventures in the U.S., Canada, Europe, and South America. On one trip, you bike through Holland; on another, you play golf in Ireland.

PHOTO EXPLORER TOURS (800-315-4462; **www.photoexplorertours.com**) focuses on photography. Although this group isn't limited to those over 50, most people who take the tour are retirees. The company, which is run by travel photographer Dennis Cox, now offers up to a dozen programs annually, which include trips to China, Tibet, and Nepal.

MALACA INSTITUTO (011-34-95-229-3242; **www.malacainst-ch.es**) organizes a special two-week vacation program for seniors who want to improve their Spanish. Lessons in "practical" Spanish are combined with cooking lessons, museum visits, dance classes, and more.

go back to *school*

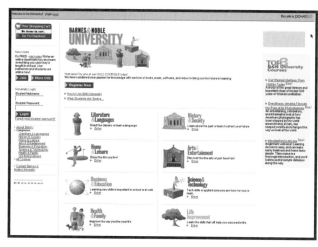

You're never too old to learn

ALTHOUGH YOU MAY BE FAR from "college age," most universities have a lot to offer students who are retired. You can take college courses in any subject that interests you—without having to matriculate toward a degree. Some regular college courses, however, do have prerequisites. That is, to take a more advanced course, such as Understanding Shakespeare and His Times, you may have to take other, more basic, courses first.

If you'd like to earn a degree, you can, of course. There's no age limitation on working toward a college diploma or even an advanced degree. Many retirees, though, are just interested in expanding their horizons—not going for a cap and gown. Your best bet, then, are courses offered through the college's continuing education department. These classes can be taken for credit (but aren't always), have fewer prerequisites, and are geared toward returning students—both young and older—who attend school simply because they want to learn more about ecology, or the Romantic poets, or Aristotle's philosophy.

If money is an issue, check out your local high schools. Many of them offer adult education courses which are generally lower in cost. And some colleges allow you to "audit" courses for a small fee. As an auditor, you can't participate in the discussions, but you can listen to the exchange, and of course, enjoy the lectures.

If traveling to and from campus is a problem, some universities now offer online courses, complete with chat rooms and teacher conferences. In fact, if you want to take courses from a famous university in another part of the country, online courses may give you the opportunity to do so. For free courses, check the listings on **www.bnuniversity.com**, sponsored by Barnes & Noble. You'll be most successful with online study if you enjoy learning by reading and writing rather than by listening. It also helps if you are self-motivated, and, of course, you must be comfortable with your computer.

ASK THE EXPERTS

I've heard about these Institutes for Learning in Retirement. What makes their offerings different from other continuing education classes?

For starters, there are absolutely no prerequisites (except for a love of learning); no credit is given; no tests or grades either; and obviously, these courses won't lead to a degree. What's more, the prices are downright cheap. At some schools, you pay $75 to $100 per term (for as many courses as you want to take during that time period) or about $25 per course. For more information, ask about an Institute for Learning in Retirement (ILR) at your local college or university.

Who teaches ILR classes?

Most institutes rely on volunteer "moderators." Often, these moderators are retired teachers who may be teaching a subject they love—but not one they necessarily taught professionally. At one college, for instance, a retired professor of pharmacology teaches a course in classical music.

GIVE BACK

Want to go back to school—as a teacher? Consider RE-SEED. That's Retirees Enhancing Science Education Through Experiments and Demonstration (617-373-8388; **www.reseed.neu.edu**). This Northeastern University program prepares engineers, scientists, and others with a science background to assist middle-school teachers in teaching physical science one day per week for a year.

now what do I do?

Answers to common questions

My wife and I both love to read. In fact, we have stacks of books that we haven't had time to read. But she says that won't keep us occupied during our retirement. I disagree. Who's right?

In some ways, you both are. While it's great that you both share the same interest, reading is a rather solitary interest that probably won't sustain you day after day. To make it work, you need to "expand" the concept. How about joining or forming a book club with others? Or perhaps you might take a literary trip that tours some of the sites mentioned by an author you both enjoy.

I was looking forward to volunteering in my local elementary school after I retired from my job as a teacher. But after a few months, I found that I resented working as a volunteer for the same tasks that I used to get paid for. Any suggestions?

While some people are happy to volunteer the expertise and skill that they honed on the job, many other retirees feel as you do. Look for a paid position that lets you use your teaching skills, and then volunteer to do work that is unrelated to your former job. You're not likely to have the same problem volunteering to address envelopes or answer phones, for example, for the American Lung Association.

I'm not able to get around easily because of my arthritic knees, but I really like to be with people. Is there any way I can join in senior activities in my community?

Make an appointment with a social worker who specializes in caring for older people. You will be surprised to find that she may have access to transportation services for seniors that could get you to many events, such as concerts and lectures at local universities, activities at community centers, and classes at your local Y.

I've been dying to travel when I retire, but now that we have the time, my wife doesn't want to. She says it's too much trouble to get someone to look after our cats, and she hates packing, and she doesn't like to fly. I'm so disappointed.

Perhaps your wife, seeing how much you'd like to travel, wouldn't mind if you went on trips without her once in a while. You could travel with groups such as Elderhostel (see page 83) if you don't want to be absolutely on your own. But discuss how she would feel being at home alone. She might like to have a friend come to stay with her while you are away.

My husband just started using a wheelchair and is worried we won't be able to travel anymore. How can I convince him otherwise?

There are many organizations to help make traveling a breeze for the disabled. Check these sources for options:

- Access-Able Travel Source (303-232-2979; www.access-able.com)
- Disabled Directory (44 0 1383 823420; www.disabilityworld.com)
- Global Access Disabled Travel Network (www.geocities.com/paris/1502)
- Accessible Vacation Home Exchange (468 840 4200; www.independentliving.org/vacationhomeswap.htm)
- Accessible Journeys (800-846-4537; www.disabilitytravel.com)
- Accessible Tours (800-533-5343; www.travel-cruises.com)
- Flying Wheels (800-535-6790)

NOW WHERE DO I GO?!

CONTACTS	BOOKS
www.aarp.org Contains information about everything from volunteer programs to life transitions to money and work issues.	**How to Retire Happy** By Stan Hinden
www.career-planning.com Offers online career planning and career counseling. Includes an online career planning test to assess your interests and capabilities.	**What Do You Want to Do When You Grow Up: Starting the Next Chapter of Your Life** By Dorothy Cantor and Andrea Thompson
www.myseniors.com Features information on travel, money, shopping, entertainment, lifestyle, and more.	**101 Secrets for a Great Retirement: Practical, Inspirational, and Fun Ideas for the Best Years of Your Life** By Mary Helen Smith and Shuford Smith
www.Freedom.goGrrl.com Offers articles on leisure and retirement for boomers and seniors.	

CHAPTER SIX

Social *Security*

Time to start collecting **92**
How much can you expect to get?

When to start taking your benefits **94**
Are there advantages in doing it earlier? Or later?

Applying for benefits **96**
When you're ready to set the process in motion

Taxes on your benefits **98**
Uncle Sam can reduce your monthly check

Social Security and your family **100**
Who else will benefit from your earned credits?

Now what do I do? **102**
Answers to common questions

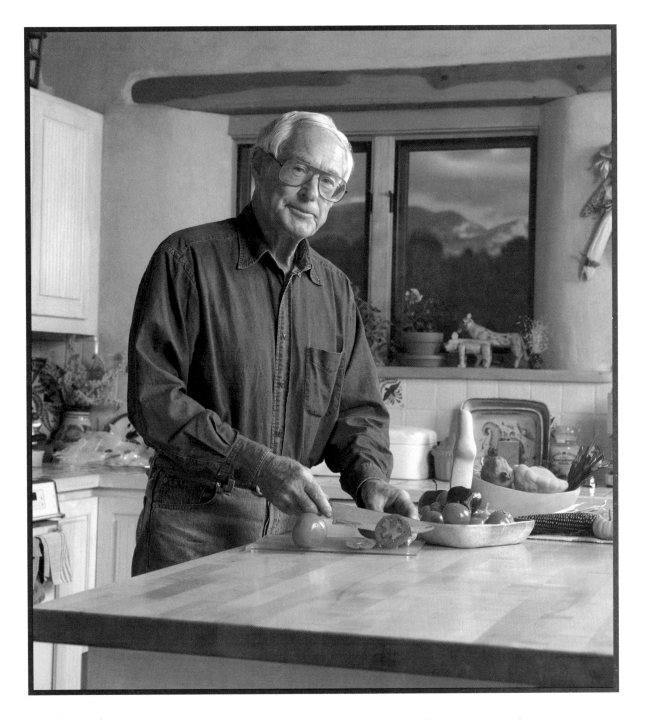

I want to continue working after I retire. Will my salary affect my Social Security payment?

time to start *collecting*

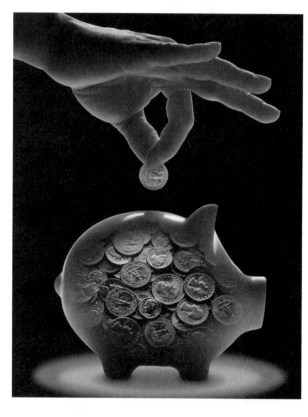

Provide the financial base for your retirement

SOCIAL SECURITY. DID YOU EVER THINK you'd see the day when this was more than just another paycheck deduction? When it would actually start to improve your cash flow? Well, with retirement, the time is here at long last.

To be eligible, you or your spouse need to have accumulated 40 **credits** during your working years. (You earn up to 4 of these credits per year of work, so most people qualify within 10 years of full-time employment.) For most people, their Social Security benefit is calculated using an average of their highest 35 years of earnings. Non-working widows and widowers of qualified working spouses can receive up to 50% of their deceased spouses' benefits.

While you have no say in the amount of benefits you are due, you can decide about what age you would like to start collecting benefits. Generally speaking, the sooner you start taking it (the earliest age you're eligible is 62), the smaller your benefit will be. The longer you delay (up to the age of 70), the bigger it'll be, but the longer you'll have to live in order for it to make economic sense.

ASK THE EXPERTS

How much can I expect to get?

The amount of your monthly check will be based on your birth date, the age you start collecting, and the average amount of money you have earned over your lifetime. There is a limit on benefits. In 2001, for example, it was $1,536 per month for someone at full retirement age. (And yes, in some cases your Social Security can be taxed. See page 98 for more.) To see how much you'll get, look at your Personal Earnings & Benefit Estimate Statement (PES), which the Social Security Administration annually mails to everyone over age 25. This shows how much in annual Social Security benefits you'll get if you **1.** retire early, **2.** retire late, **3.** retire at your normal retirement age, or **4.** become disabled.

I didn't get my Social Security Personal Earnings & Benefit Estimate. How do I request one?

You have several options:

- Call the SSA at 800-772-1213 to request the statement.
- Get a copy of the request form at your local Social Security office. Then fill it out and mail it in.
- Submit your request on the Social Security Administration's Web site, **www.ssa.gov**, either directly on-screen or by downloading a request form and mailing it in.

There's an error in my PES. What should I do?

If you spot a mistake, contact the SSA immediately to have their estimate adjusted. Waiting more than a year or two to correct errors can make the corrections difficult to achieve. To contact SSA:

Tel: 800-772-1213

Fax: 888-475-1000

Internet: **www.ssa.gov**

E-mail: webmaster@ssa.gov

HOW ARE BENEFITS CALCULATED

Your benefits aren't tied to how much in SS taxes you've paid. In fact, the SS taxes you've paid don't actually accumulate for your benefit—they've been used for retirement benefits of current retirees. The system is set up so that your own SS benefits will come from SS taxes paid by people who are still working when you retire.

The way your benefits are calculated is so complicated that not even your genius Uncle Mort could understand it: things like "average indexed monthly earnings," "computation years," "divisor months," "bend points," and "primary insurance amounts" go into the computation. Luckily, the computers at the Social Security Administration (SSA) do the work for you.

when to start taking your *benefits*

Waiting for full benefits

"FULL" RETIREMENT AGE USED to be 65 for everyone. But thanks to greater life expectancies, the government has moved the official year back a bit. Depending on your birthday, full retirement ranges from 65 to 67. The chart below indicates the age when you are eligible for full retirement SS benefits.

If your birthday is:	Then your "full" retirement age is:
1-1-38 or before	65
1-2-38 to 1-1-39	65 and 2 months
1-2-39 to 1-1-40	65 and 4 months
1-2-40 to 1-1-41	65 and 6 months
1-2-41 to 1-1-42	65 and 8 months
1-2-42 to 1-1-43	65 and 10 months
1-2-43 to 1-1-55	66
1-2-55 to 1-1-56	66 and 2 months
1-2-56 to 1-1-57	66 and 4 months
1-2-57 to 1-1-58	66 and 6 months
1-2-58 to 1-1-59	66 and 8 months
1-2-59 to 1-1-60	66 and 10 months
After 1-1-60	67

You can start your SS benefits as early as age 62. But there's a catch: The amount you get each month will be 20% to 30% less than if you wait until your full retirement age.

You can delay your benefits, too. The longer you wait, the higher your monthly benefit is likely to be. Depending on your year of birth, the amount will be 3% to 8% more per year than it would be at full retirement. (Once you turn 70, the amount won't keep increasing, but you can still file for benefits.)

ⒶSK THE EXPERTS

I don't know what to do—should I take my Social Security early or wait until I reach full retirement?

Here are some things to consider when making this decision.

1. Your health and life expectancy. If you're healthy and your family routinely lives into the triple digits, delaying SS could be beneficial, since you'll probably have ample years of higher earning to make up for taking fewer total payments. On the other hand, if you are in poor health, taking SS benefits earlier and maximizing the number of payments you receive might make the most sense.

2. Your work situation. If you keep working after you retire, taking early benefits could cost you. How? If you earn more than $10,000 a year, your benefits will be reduced $1 for every $2 you earn above the limit, until you reach full retirement age (see page 99).

3. Your marital status. If you have a younger spouse with low earnings, waiting as long as possible might be in his or her best interest because it will ensure a greater income source to them, even after you have passed away.

4. Your feelings. Some people simply feel more comfortable starting their retirement benefits as soon as possible, even if it means less total income overall. If you feel it's best to take the "bird in hand," then go for it.

applying for *benefits*

SO, YOU'VE DECIDED TO take the leap and apply for Social Security benefits. That's great! Now what?

First, try to apply at least three months before you want your benefits to start, because it takes at least eight weeks for your application to be processed. If you're not sure whether to apply early, on time, or delayed, or if you have other questions or concerns, contacting the SSA six months early is a good idea.

The checks won't start coming until you've signed up

When you sign up for Social Security at age 65, you will automatically be enrolled in Medicare. If you don't plan to apply for SS by your 65th birthday, contact the Social Security Association for Medicare enrollment at least three months before you turn 65 and apply for Medicare separately.

There are several ways to apply for Social Security benefits: over the phone, in person, or online. To prevent delays, avoid filing more than one application (online *and* over the phone, for instance).

- Call 800-772-1213 to schedule a time to apply over the phone.
- Call 800-772-1213 to schedule a time to apply at a nearby Social Security office.
- To apply for benefits online, go to the Social Security Web site: **www.ssa.gov/applytoretire**.
- You can't apply for benefits by mail, but you can write for assistance. Address your questions to: SSA, Office of Public Inquiries, 6401 Security Blvd., Room 4-C-D Annex, Baltimore, MD 21235.

ASK THE EXPERTS

What documents do I need to have on hand before I can apply for Social Security?

Get ready for a shock. The examiners at the Social Security office will need to check all of the following documents:

- Social Security number
- Original birth certificate
- Original W-2 forms or self-employment tax return for the last two years
- Military discharge papers
- Spouse's birth certificate and Social Security number
- Proof of U.S. citizenship or lawful alien status (if you weren't born in the U.S.)
- Bank account name and number (so your benefits can be directly deposited into your account)
- A marriage certificate if you are applying for benefits based on your spouse's earnings
- A death certificate if you and your family want to apply for survivor's benefits

---

TIMELY TIP: WHEN TO GO

Plan your visit to the local SSA office at the end of a month, going three and a half months before your full retirement date if necessary. Why? Most checks are paid the first few days of the month, and people usually request lost/replacement checks the first two weeks of the month, so you'll probably sit in the waiting room longer if you go early in the month. And avoid lunchtime visits, since there are more working people looking for help—and fewer aides there to give it.

taxes on your *benefits*

OKAY, NOW FOR THE BAD NEWS. The Social Security benefits you receive may be subject to federal income taxes. The amount of your Social Security benefit that will be taxed depends on your adjusted gross income, including *half* of your Social Security benefit, and any tax-exempt dividends or interest. **Adjusted gross income** is your income after you've taken certain deductions, such as retirement plan contributions, alimony, and moving expenses.

If you owe taxes on your Social Security benefits, you will need to pay them in **estimated quarterly payments** (see page 32) or have the amount of tax you owe withheld from your Social Security check. Although you'll get a smaller check each month, you won't have to remember to make your quarterly payments. It's kind of like the old days of getting a paycheck with the taxes already taken out.

The amount depends on your other sources of income

An estimation of the federal taxes on your Social Security benefits appears below:

ESTIMATING TAXES ON SOCIAL SECURITY BENEFITS

Income including one-half of your Social Security benefits		Tax Consequences on benefits:
If you're single	If you're married	
Up to $25,000	Up to $32,000	Social Security not taxed
Between $25,000 and $34,000	Between $32,000 and $44,000	50% of Social Security taxed
Over $34,000	Over $44,000	Up to 85% of Social Security taxed

ⒶSK THE EXPERTS

I want to continue working after I retire. Will my salary affect my Social Security payment?

It depends. As of January 2000, once you reach your full retirement age, you can earn as much as you want without anything being deducted from your Social Security benefits. However, you will be penalized for working if you take benefits before your full retirement age, provided the amount you earn annually is more than $10,680 (the cap for 2001). For every $2 you earn above that amount, you will forfeit $1 in Social Security benefits. During the year you reach full retirement age, you will forfeit $1 for every $3 you earn annually over $25,000. Beginning with the month you reach full retirement, you no longer forfeit any amount, no matter how much you earn.

How can I boost my Social Security benefits?

If you delay taking your Social Security benefits after your full retirement age, you could increase the amount of benefits you eventually receive—provided your earnings remain high. Since your benefit is determined in part by an average of your highest earnings, several more high-income years could bring up that average a bit. But remember that no matter how high your income was, there is a set maximum limit to Social Security payments.

FIRST PERSON DISASTER STORY

Giving Money Back to Uncle Sam

I wanted to retire as soon as possible (I can live on the interest from my investments), so I applied for Social Security benefits the minute I turned 62. Six months later, I was offered an interesting part-time job, paid by the hour, at the museum where I used to be a curator. I got to meet lots of fascinating people who were donors, as well as attending special events at their homes. Before I knew it, I was piling up the hours and ended up making $30,000 a year from the job. I was horrified to find that my Social Security benefits would be reduced by $1 for every $2 that I had I earned over $10,680. Since I only got $13,750 a year from Social Security, and was penalized about $9,600, it wiped out 70% of my SS benefits. I would have been smarter to wait until I was 65 to take my Social Security benefits. Then I could have earned as much as I wanted with no penalty, and my Social Security checks would have been about 20% fatter as well.

—George L., New York, New York

social security and your *family*

Who else might receive checks based on your benefits?

YOU MAY NOT BE THE ONLY ONE who reaps Social Security rewards from your lifetime of slaving away. Your spouse may be at an advantage if *half* your benefit amount is higher than her full benefit amount. At age 62, your non-working spouse is entitled to a reduced benefit (37.5% of your full benefit). If she waits until her full retirement age, she will be entitled to 50% of your full benefit. She is entitled to this benefit regardless of whether you are still working and not claiming benefits yet or if you have died. (The same benefits apply to your unmarried ex-spouse, provided your marriage lasted more than 10 years, during which you worked and earned your Social Security credits.)

Social Security also helps your family after you die. Your spouse will continue to get Social Security, based on your benefit amount. (If your spouse worked, Social Security will base your benefits on the higher amount of the two of you.) Your ex-spouse will still continue to collect on your Social Security after you die. And thanks to your working years, Social Security will pay monthly survivor benefits to any minor children (under age 19), and any disabled children age 18 or older. Even your elderly parents are covered, provided they have been dependent upon you for at least half of their financial support.

By the way, if you're retiring and your current and/or ex-spouse has substantially higher lifetime earnings than you, you may be able to boost your own benefit by making a claim on his or her account.

DISABILITY INSURANCE

If you're not yet at full retirement age but become fully disabled, you may receive benefits from Social Security through Social Security Disability Insurance. Like Social Security, the amount you receive will be based on the number of credits you have earned and the amount of money you made during your working years. Start the application process immediately after you are told you won't be able to work again, because the approval process sometimes takes months. If you are turned down on your first try, you may want to gather more medical evidence and try again.

Disability Insurance from Social Security does not apply if you become disabled *after* you reach full retirement age. See long-term care insurance (page 152) and Medicare (page 142) for additional information.

now what do I do?

Answers to common questions

If I delay taking my Social Security benefits past full retirement age, will my Medicare benefits be delayed, too?

No. Even if you decide to delay your retirement benefits, you can—and generally should—sign up for Medicare at age 65.

I've worked for many years, but my Social Security statement doesn't reflect any of my earnings. What happened?

There are a number of people who aren't covered by Social Security. These include federal employees hired before 1984; workers covered under the Railroad Retirement System; state employees covered under their own retirement system; many school system employees with their own programs; and certain clergy who elect not to participate in Social Security. If you're not covered, you probably haven't had SS taxes withheld from your paycheck, but check with the SSA to be sure.

My husband passed away several years ago, and I'm thinking about remarrying. How will this impact my Social Security benefits?

It depends. If you're already collecting as a widow on your deceased husband's account, your benefits will not change when you remarry. However, if you are just now preparing to file for widow's benefits (you are eligible at age 60), file before you get remarried—otherwise you won't be eligible for the benefits.

When will I receive my check each month?

Checks are paid once a month, in arrears. For example, your payment for your April benefits will arrive in May, depending on your birthday:

IF YOUR BIRTHDAY IS:	YOUR PAYMENT IS MADE:
1st through 10th of the month	2nd Wednesday of each month
11th through 20th of the month	3rd Wednesday of each month
21st through 31st of the month	4th Wednesday of each month

To access your money as soon as possible, sign up for the government's direct deposit program when you apply. Funds will be posted to your checking account and available to you the same day.

If I've earned a million dollars, will my Social Security benefit reflect that?

The Social Security Administration has set a maximum income level (which increases slightly every year due to inflation). Once you exceed that level, the benefit paid by Social Security stays the same. For example, if billionaire Bill Gates (born in 1955) starts taking Social Security benefits at age 66, the amount he gets will be exactly the same as that received by all other people born that year whose lifetime earnings are at least at the maximum level.

I've worked a total of nine years. Do I qualify for Social Security benefits?

No, not unless you're married and your spouse qualifies, and you can secure benefits under his or her earnings. The criterion for qualifying is 40 credits, and you can't earn more than 4 credits per year, regardless of how much money you have made. That's why it's important to review your Social Security Earnings & Benefit Estimate before you retire. Working one more year could make all the difference toward a happy retirement.

NOW WHERE DO I GO?!

WEB ADDRESSES	BOOKS
www.ssa.gov (800-772-1213) www.socialsecurity.com/opening.html	**Benefits Handbook** By Stanley A. Tomkiel III

401(k)s and pensions

Your 401 (k) 106
How much have you got in there?

401 (k): Lump-sum distribution 108
Better know what you're doing

401 (k): Leave it with your employer . . 110
The 401(k) can act like an IRA

401 (k): Required distributions 112
When to take your money out

Your SEP, SIMPLE, or Keogh 114
If you have one of these retirement saving plans

Your pension 116
If your company has a plan, you may have
benefits

Pension: Annuity payments 118
Choosing the right type is key

Pension: Lump-sum payment 120
Treat it just like a lump sum from your 401(k)

Now what do I do? 122
Answers to common questions

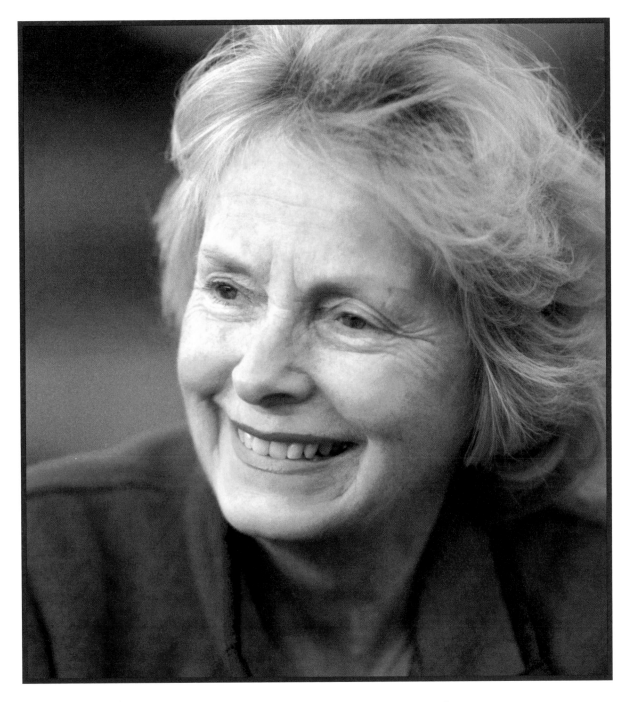

66 *I'm afraid I'll run out of money. How much can I safely withdraw from my 401(k) each year?* 99

your
401(k)

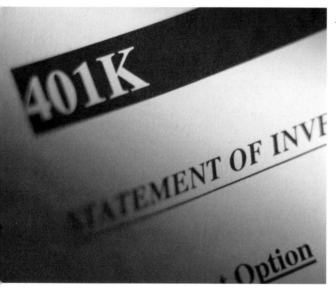

How much is in there?

FINALLY YOU'RE RETIRING, AND it's time to start withdrawing the money from your 401(k). Hurrah! How much have you got in there anyway? It depends on these factors:

● **THE AMOUNT OF MONEY YOU CONTRIBUTED FROM EACH PAYCHECK AND THE NUMBER OF YEARS YOU CONTRIBUTED TO THE PLAN:** You, the employee, saved a fixed percentage of your weekly paycheck in a tax-deferred retirement savings account. But you may have saved less than the maximum. You may have changed the percentage during your working years or gone without making a contribution part of the time. If you got in a pinch, you may even have had to borrow from your account, which means less was invested, so less was earned. Those decisions were left up to you. Now you will find they have affected the amount in your account.

● **THE SIZE OF YOUR EMPLOYER'S CONTRIBUTION (IF ANY):** Your company may have made contributions to your account as well, depending on the company's policy. For every pretax dollar you contributed (up to a certain percentage), your employer may have kicked in anywhere from $.25 to $1.00 (referred to as the **matching amount**).

● **THE TYPES OF INVESTMENTS YOU PICKED AND HOW THOSE INVESTMENTS PERFORMED OVER TIME:** The 401(k) allows some discretion in how your account is invested. The amount your account has earned is dependent in part on how well those investments performed over the years.

● **DON'T FORGET ABOUT TAXES:** Your 401(k) contribution was made with pretax dollars. That means the money was deducted from your paycheck before taxes were withdrawn. And you've paid no taxes so far on what your 401(k) account has earned. The manner in which you take the money out of your account will determine how and when you eventually pay the taxes on the money.

WHAT'S A 403(b) PLAN?

If you work for a non-profit hospital, a school, or a government agency, you probably have a 403(b) plan instead of a 401(k). The plans are similar, but check with your financial adviser or accountant to find out exactly how you should take withdrawals in retirement.

Ask THE EXPERTS

Doesn't all the money in my 401(k) account belong to me?

It depends. That part of the money you contributed from your paycheck, and its earnings, are yours—period. It doesn't matter if you worked for the company for five weeks or five years. The matching contribution that your employer kicked in, however, is a different matter. This money isn't yours until you are **vested**, or officially entitled to it. Many employers allow you to vest in increments over a period of seven years; some offer immediate vesting. Others vest you all at once, but after a set period of time. Check with your employee benefits office about the vesting requirements for receiving the company's contributions before you make any retirement decisions.

Could a former employer owe me any money?

Yes, if you've switched jobs and left your 401(k) account invested with a previous employer, you're entitled to the amount you contributed and the money it has continued to earn. Contact your former company's benefits department and see what's coming to you.

I am so tempted to take the money and buy a round-the-world trip. Is this a good way to spend it?

Not unless you want to get hit with a huge tax bill. There are rules about when you can begin taking out 401(k) money, as well as how much you should take out in order to avoid tax problems.

401(k):
lump-sum distribution

*Get your
hands on
that money*

OVER THE YEARS, YOU'VE REGULARLY SOCKED away those pretax dollars into your 401(k) account. Good work! You can now reap the rewards. Whether it's worth $10,000 or $1 million, those retirement savings are finally yours. It's time to think about how you're going to take it out. Most people take it in one lump sum. The careful ones consider the tax consequences. Read on and find out.

TAKE THE MONEY-AND RUN This idea sounds better than it actually is. Why? When you take a lump-sum payment, you get all of the money at once, within one tax year. Trouble is, you have to pay all the income tax due on that money in the same tax year, so you'll have to fork over a hefty chunk of your savings to the government almost immediately. What's more, the tax-deferred earnings on your money will stop.

TAKE THE MONEY-AND ROLL IT INTO AN IRA This strategy generally makes the most sense. When you roll your 401(k) distribution into an Individual Retirement Account (see page 128), your money can continue to grow tax-deferred. You maintain control over the money, investing your account as aggressively or as conservatively as you want. And you can tap into the money as needed.

LEAVE IT WITH YOUR COMPANY—AND DON'T DO A THING If you leave the money in your 401(k) until you make a final decision, the company's investment firm will continue to invest it according to your wishes, and you can withdraw what you want, when you want (see page 110). Just make sure your spouse and heirs know about the account.

HOW DO I ROLL OVER MY 401(k)?

You have several options. But the IRS has some sticky rules. Be prepared for some paperwork and a short time frame (60 days) within which you need to complete the task.

1) DO IT DIRECTLY: Tell your employer to deposit your lump sum directly into a new or an existing IRA, if you already have one set up. For a direct rollover, your employer will ask you to fill out an instruction form indicating exactly where the money should go, such as to a particular mutual fund. The advantages: You beat the IRS requirement that says your employer must deduct a withholding tax from your lump sum, because the check isn't made out to you, it's made out to the institution. In many cases, the check will be sent directly to your house, in which case you'll need to mail it to your IRA's custodian. As long as this check is made out to the IRA account, it'll be considered a "direct rollover."

2) DO IT YOURSELF WITHIN 60 DAYS: Your employer hands over a lump-sum check to you. Now you've got 60 days to roll over the money into an IRA. The disadvantages: Since the check is made out to you, your employer must deduct 20% mandatory withholding tax, which means you'll only have a check for 80% of your money. You'll eventually get a refund for that 20%, of course, when you file your tax return. But meanwhile, during the 60-day rollover time limit, you'll have to add the missing 20% out of your own pocket *or that 20% will be taxed as income*. Another drawback: Miss that 60-day deadline, even by a hair, and you'll owe tax on the *entire amount*.

3) CONVERT IT TO A ROTH IRA: This is a bit tricky. First, you roll your 401(k) fund into a traditional IRA. Then you convert that IRA into a Roth (see page 132). There are no limits on the amount you can convert, but there are eligibility limits based on income. If you convert, you may want to do it in smaller increments because the taxes that you will have to pay upon conversion can strain your cash flow. But from that point on, all of your withdrawals, both principal and interest, will generally be completely free from income tax. Why convert? Because you have a lot of retirement funding and you don't want to bother with mandatory withdrawals, and the whole Roth IRA can be left to your heirs income tax free.

401(k): leave it with your employer

If their 401(k) plan is giving you good returns, let the money stay there

IT'S TRUE, MANY PEOPLE PREFER to take all their 401(k) money with them at retirement. But you do have another, very smart option: Just leave your 401(k) where it is. Here are several reasons why it might make sense for you:

YOU DON'T WANT TO MAKE FURTHER INVESTMENT DECISIONS RIGHT NOW. Perhaps you like the way the funds in your company plan are performing, or you enjoy the investment options offered by your plan. Why reinvent the wheel by taking the money out and then spending time looking for a suitable investment for it somewhere else?

YOU WANT YOUR MONEY TO CONTINUE TO GROW TAX-DEFERRED. Leaving the money in your employer's plan has no immediate tax consequences. Your money will keep growing tax-deferred. You'll only pay tax on the money as you withdraw it, the same as with an IRA.

YOU'RE UNSURE ABOUT WHAT TO DO WITH YOUR MONEY. Doing nothing can be okay in this instance, while you take the time to think things over. Leave your money in your 401(k) account . . . and mull over your options for a few months. Should you decide a month from now—or several years from now—that you want to roll the money into an IRA, you can do so at that time.

ASK THE EXPERTS

I'd like to receive a monthly income from my 401 (k). How do I do that?

Here are two ways to do it:

1. Take a lump-sum distribution and roll it immediately into an IRA. You can then take monthly payments—or more or less frequent distributions—as you see fit. For example, a mutual fund company (when acting as the custodian of your Rollover IRA) will let you set up an automatic distribution plan. That is, they'll automatically mail you a monthly check.

2. Ask your company to set up an installment payment schedule. Your employer (or the mutual fund that manages the company's 401(k) plan) will essentially use your money to pay you a set monthly amount immediately. (These are called **annuitized distributions**.) This guarantees you a fixed income for the rest of your life.

I like the idea of getting annuitized distributions from my company, but is it the best way to go?

Ask your financial planner or accountant about the long-term implications. An annuitized distribution is safe, and it's easy—you don't have to lift a finger to get your money. However, an annuity is not generally the most economical choice, because it offers no protection against **inflation** (the rising cost of living). Rolling over the money into an IRA is considered a better bet because the investments usually produce higher total returns than if you annuitize. Bear in mind that once you annuitize, you can't go back. That is, if you decide at some future date that rolling over the money into an IRA would have been a smarter option, you can't switch.

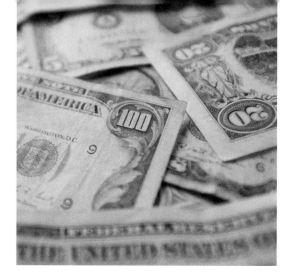

401(k): required distributions

Once you start taking them, you have to keep on taking them every year

IF YOU DIDN'T ROLL OVER THE MONEY from your 401(k) into an IRA, and you want or need to start taking money out, there are a few rules to follow. Starting at age 59½, you can take as much or as little money out of your 401(k) as you want—just know you will have to pay income tax on it. Or you can wait to start taking distributions at any year up until age 70½, when you absolutely *must* start taking something called a **required minimum distribution** (or RMD).

How is the required minimum distribution determined? Good question. Basically, your 401(k) balance is divided by a figure from a government distribution table. (It's actually an actuarial table based on the life expectancy of you and your beneficiary.) Here's another rule: Once you start taking your RMDs, you cannot stop. Every year thereafter, you have to take at least your minimum distribution. You can, of course, take out more than your required minimum distribution (see page 114). Just check with your accountant to see if the extra income will move you into an undesirable tax bracket.

The one exception to the RMD rule? If you don't retire by 70½ and continue working, you don't have to take the minimum withdrawals from your 401(k). And you can keep making contributions until the year you actually do retire—welcome news for those who want to put off their retirement.

SK THE EXPERTS

I'm 55 and want to retire early. Can I get the money out of my 401(k) early?

Yes. There is a early retirement loophole that lets you take money out starting at age 55 provided you are retiring from a job with the same company that has your 401(k).

I was laid off at 54. Can I take money out of my 401(k) without paying a penalty?

Alas, you'll get socked with a 10% early withdrawal penalty in addition to the usual income taxes—unless your withdrawal qualifies as a hardship withdrawal, such as the purchase of a new home or the cost of a college education, or a "special circumstance" such as substantial medical expenses and early retirement. Check with the IRS or your accountant first to make sure you qualify.

Your SEP, SIMPLE or *Keogh*

*Distributions work
like those for
IRAs and 401(k)s*

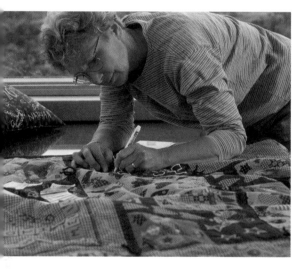

IF YOU'VE WORKED FOR SMALL COMPANIES
or been self-employed for most of your working life,
chances are you have a SEP IRA (Simplified Employee
Pension Plan), SIMPLE IRA, or Keogh retirement plan
ready and waiting for your self-appointed day of retirement. And today's the day. But how do you take the
money out? Are there rules and regulations?

Yes, whenever taxes are involved, there are rules. The distribution rules for
SEPs and SIMPLEs are fairly, well, simple. They are subject to the same
basic rules as a regular IRA. That is, you can start taking money out of
your SEP or SIMPLE when you turn age 59½—and of course, you must
pay income tax on it (usually at a lower income tax bracket now that
you've stopped working). One more rule: You must start making a
required minimum distribution (or RMD) withdrawal the year that you
turn 70½. (Technically, you have until April 1 of the year *after* you turn
70½ to begin withdrawing the funds.) As with IRAs, your RMD amount is
based on the life expectancy of you and your beneficiary.

Taking your money out of a Keogh is the same deal. Turn 59½ and you can start taking it out and paying taxes (hopefully at a lower income tax rate than when you were working). Once you turn 70½ you must start taking it out—unless you keep working. Here a Keogh is like a 401(k): If you keep working in your same line of work, you don't have to take any RMDs and in fact, you can continue to make contributions. Good news for the working diehards.

ASK THE EXPERTS

Do I have to take minimum distributions from my Simplified Employee Pension (SEP) if I'm still working?

Yes. SEP IRAs and SIMPLE IRAs operate under the same rules as regular IRAs. You must start taking money out of your account in the year that you turn 70½. It doesn't matter if you are still working or not. Uncle Sam wants his taxes paid back.

Are there any special rules for early withdrawals of SIMPLEs?

Yes. If you make an early withdrawal of funds from your SIMPLE within two years of the date that you began contributing to it, you'll have to pay an early withdrawal penalty of 25%. After two years, the penalty drops to 10%.

your *pension*

Many larger companies still offer them

AH, THE PENSION. It used to be standard for workers to receive pension payments once they retired. Now it seems more like found money. If you are **vested** (entitled to certain benefits based on years of service) and due pension money, good for you. The amount you will receive is calculated by a formula, which varies from one employer to the next. Typically, it includes factors such as the number of years you worked for the company and your final salary, or an average of your salary over a number of years when it was highest, or a flat amount per year of service.

How much you get will depend on when you retire: early, late, or at the normal retirement age. If you're retiring early (after a long career with the company), for instance, your pension benefits may be reduced because you'll now be receiving them over a longer period of time. And if you've been with the firm for just a few years (after job-hopping most of your career), your pension benefits may not amount to much at all.

How much you get will also depend on how you collect your pension benefits once you retire. Some companies allow you to take the money in one lump sum and invest it yourself (see pages 120-121), or as an annuity, collecting a monthly check from the company for the rest of your life (see pages 132-133).

SK THE EXPERTS

Do I have to worry about vesting?

Absolutely. In order to collect a pension, you must be fully vested (that is, eligible to receive pension benefits) in your company's plan. How do you become eligible? Companies have different vesting schedules. With some firms, you're vested immediately upon employment; with others, you're vested gradually over a period of years (known as graded vesting), or all at once after a certain time period has elapsed, say five years (known as cliff vesting). If you are not fully vested, some companies offer to vest you as an incentive to take early retirement. Check with your employee benefits office to find out about your company's vesting schedule.

I keep hearing about defined benefits. What does that mean?

It means that the amount you receive from your pension plan is a set amount for the rest of your life. An annuity-type distribution is considered a defined benefit plan.

Are taxes taken out of my pension check?

In most cases, the money that you receive from your pension is considered taxable income. That means, obviously, that you must pay income tax on the money. Will those taxes be taken directly from your monthly check? It depends on your particular plan. Plans typically withhold taxes from your check, but you can usually opt not to have the taxes withheld. In the latter case, you'll then have to pay those taxes yourself, on an annual or quarterly basis. Before you retire and start drawing your pension, ask about the tax implications of your particular plan and what arrangements, if any, are made for tax withholding.

pension annuity payments

Choosing the right type may be tricky

IF YOU DECIDE TO TAKE YOUR ANNUAL PENSION benefits in a monthly annuity distribution, you'll have to make one more big decision: You must choose between a **single-life annuity** (the payments stop when you die) or a **joint and survivor annuity**. (You get a smaller monthly income, but it continues to be paid to your spouse after your death.)

Before you decide, ask your company's pension office for an estimate of both amounts, and discuss the issue with your spouse and your financial adviser. Keep in mind that your choice is generally irrevocable. That means once you retire and start receiving pension benefits of one type, you can't then ask the company to change to the other type of payment.

Single-Life Annuity This provides a monthly amount to you alone, the retiree, for life. When you pick this option, your monthly payments will be larger because the benefits are based on your life expectancy alone. The downside: Your spouse will be left with no income from your pension when you die. If you're not married, then you should take the single-life option and get the higher payments. If you and your spouse each have solid pensions of your own—and your spouse won't have to depend on your pension for support after you die—then, again, go with the larger, single-life annuity. But if your spouse might need that pension money after you die, then select the joint and survivor annuity.

Joint and Survivor Annuity This type of payment provides a monthly income to you, the retiree. When you die, however, your pension keeps on issuing monthly payments to your spouse for the rest of his or her life. The drawback: You get less money each month than you would with the single-life option because your pension benefit must now be spread over the life expectancy of two people.

RED FLAG

Your spouse is entitled to survivor rights to your pension. In most cases, that means when you die your spouse will get at least half the pension benefit that you were receiving. When you elect a single-life option, however, you waive that right. Under most plans, your spouse must sign an agreement form indicating that he or she consents to the terms of a single-life annuity.

SK THE EXPERTS

What's the better choice: Single-Life or Joint and Survivor?

The answer depends on your personal situation. Married women are typically advised to take single-life payment on their own pensions because women generally outlive men. Conversely, husbands are often advised to take the joint and survivor option on their pensions because statistics indicate that their wives will probably outlive them. With this arrangement, the husband gets less money each month than he would with the single-life option. When the husband dies, his spouse will get a monthly payment for the rest of her life. But the surviving spouse does not get as much as the retiree received during his life. The surviving spouse generally gets 50% of the original benefit.

Can I name my child as my beneficiary?

The joint and survivor option is for your spouse only. If you are widowed or single, you may be able to take other options. (Again, this depends on your plan.) One such option is called a Guaranteed Payment Annuity, which lets you pick another family member as beneficiary.

I'm divorced. Am I entitled to half of my ex-husband's pension?

A pension is a marital asset, so if pension payments were not stipulated in your divorce proceedings, you can't get them now.

FIRST PERSON   DISASTER STORY

Sometimes Conventional Wisdom Doesn't Work

When I retired five years ago, I chose the joint and survivor benefit for my pension. It was the conventional thing to do. I didn't take my wife's poor health into consideration. I guess I always assumed she would outlive me, and so I wanted to provide for her. She passed away last year, and now I'm stuck with these lower benefits for the rest of my life. I wish I had thought about the decision a bit harder and taken the single-life option. An old colleague of mine told me that not only should I have taken the single-life option, but I could have used the extra money from the higher payment to help continue to make payments on my whole-life insurance policy. That way, if I died first, my wife would collect on the policy. And if she died first, I could cancel the policy and I'd still be getting the higher pension payments. Live and learn.

—Sam S., Cleveland, Ohio

pension: lump-sum payment

Invested well, it can protect against inflation

WHEN YOU RETIRE, YOUR EMPLOYER may offer to give you your pension in one single check. This is called a **lump-sum payment.** Instead of getting a monthly income paid for the rest of your life, you get the entire amount rolled over into a separate or existing IRA. Then it becomes your job to invest the money—and/or spend it—as you see fit.

The amount you get is calculated using a slightly different formula than the monthly payment plan. It's based on the following: the amount of the single-life annuity; the retiree's age; and an interest rate, determined by the plan, that will convert your possible future pension income into a current market value.

Not all pensions offer this alternative. But if your pension plan does, you'll want to consider the following:

● Can you invest that money wisely (or perhaps pay someone to do it for you)? Lump sums make sense for people who believe that they can earn more by investing their money themselves than they would have otherwise received in monthly annuity payments.

● How badly do you think inflation will erode your savings? A lump-sum payment invested partially in stocks should protect your money against rising prices. Most annuities offer no such protection.

Talk to a financial planner or an accountant who can run the numbers for you. Before you can make an intelligent decision, you need to see how each choice stacks up over the long term.

PENSION CHECKLIST

Important questions to ask your company benefits administrator about your pension plan:

- Is the pension plan "integrated" with your Social Security benefits? Under this arrangement, your monthly pension income would be reduced once you start collecting Social Security benefits. The amount of your monthly Social Security benefit would be subtracted from your original pension benefit, and you would receive the reduced monthly amount from the company.
- How will your benefits be calculated? Different plans use different formulas. A **unit benefit formula,** for instance, typically works like this: 1% to 2% multiplied by your final average compensation (which is usually your average compensation over the highest 3 or 5 years within the last 10 years, but it could also be your career average compensation) multiplied by your years of service. A **fixed benefit formula**, on the other hand, usually works this way: After 25 years of service, you get 50% of your final average compensation.
- If you retire early—even two years early—will your benefits be affected? If so, by how much? The pension plan administrator will usually give you comparative estimates a few years before your full retirement date.
- At retirement, can you take your payment as a lump sum or as an annuity with monthly payments? Not all companies offer the option of a lump-sum payout. (If your pension benefit is small, will it be paid annually instead of monthly?)
- Are your benefits going to be adjusted for inflation? Less than 10% of corporate pension plans adjust annuity payments for inflation. When making a decision whether to collect your pension as a lump sum for you to invest, you'll have to consider that, by investing a part of it in equities, you can make up for the rate of inflation. Your financial adviser can determine how much should be put into equities to make this happen.

IN CASE QUESTIONS ARISE IN THE FUTURE

You will need to know the name of your pension plan, the Employer Identification Number (EIN) and the plan's number (PN). Why? It makes applying for your pension a snap. Also, sometimes companies merge and pensions can get lost in the shuffle. If you've "lost" your pension, contact the Pension Benefit Guaranty Corp. at 800-400-7242 or **www. pbgc.gov.**

now what do I do?

Answers to common questions

My company lost several of its key clients in the past two years. If my company goes out of business or declares bankruptcy, will I lose my pension benefits?
Probably not. Until 1974, there was little or no protection for pensions. But thanks to the Employee Retirement Income Security Act (ERISA), most pension plans are now insured by the federal government through the Pension Benefit Guaranty Corporation (PBGC). If your employer goes out of business or cannot afford to pay your retirement benefits, PBGC will pay your benefits, up to certain limits. In most cases, though, the PBGC guarantee covers all of the earned benefits.

I can't decide if I should take my pension in a lump sum or as a monthly payment. What do most people do?
Everyone's situation is slightly different, but here are two general rules of thumb: 1) If you're an experienced investor, or if you work with a good financial planner, consider the lump sum. The interest rates offered by company-sponsored annuities generally aren't that competitive, and you can do better by investing the lump sum. 2) If you're an inexperienced investor or have no trusted financial adviser, consider the monthly pension. Yes, you might be able to earn more by investing the money yourself, but then again, you might not. At least with the pension, you know what you're getting—and it's for life.

I'm a doctor working in a not-for-profit hospital. I've always contributed to our hospital's 403(b) plan, which works something like a 401(k). Are the rules for mandatory withdrawals the same?

Not necessarily. There were no withdrawal rules when 403(b) plans were first set up. But the Tax Reform Act of 1986 decreed that 403(b)s should have distribution rules like 401(k) plans. In other words, you must start taking money out at age 70½. There are some loopholes in this new ruling, though, which might allow you to defer withdrawals until age 75. Check with a financial planner or a pension expert.

I'm afraid that I'll run out of money eventually. How much can I safely withdraw from my 401(k) each year?

How much you can safely withdraw—without fear of depleting all your funds—depends on a number of factors, such as your other sources of retirement income, your life expectancy, and your general living expenses. (See page 30.) Some recent studies have found, however, that you'd be pretty safe if your annual withdrawal is no more than 4% of the value of your 401(k).

NOW WHERE DO I GO?!

WEB ADDRESSES

www.aoa.dhhs.gov/factsheets/pension.html
The Administration on Aging offers information about pensions and "pension counseling programs" to help you obtain the correct information about your pension plan.

www.401K.com
A Fidelity site, it answers many questions about 401(k) plans.

www.lifeadvice.com
MetLife offers information on a variety of personal finance topics, such as "401(k) Plans" and "Planning for Retirement."

www.quicken.com
A compendium of understandable personal finance information. Click on "retirement."

BOOKS

IRAs, 401(k)s & Other Retirement Plans: Taking Your Money Out
by Twila Slesnick, Ph.D., Enrolled Agent and Attorney John C. Suttle, CPA

The Complete Idiot's Guide to 401(k) Plans
by Wayne G. Bogosian and Dee Lee

A Commonsense Guide to Your 401(k)
by Mary Rowland

Making the Most of Your 401(k)
by Gordon K. Williamson

dealing with *IRAs*

Your accounts and taxes 126
Many types, all serving different purposes

Individual Retirement Accounts 128
A basic repository for retirement assets

IRAs: Distribution and taxes 130
Once you start taking money out, you can't skip a year

Roth IRAs 132
A flexible retirement account

Annuities 134
Half insurance policy, half IRA

Now what do I do? 136
Answers to common questions

How do we go about beginning the withdrawal process for our IRAs?

your
accounts and
taxes

Each type serves a different purpose

IF YOU'VE DECIDED TO RETIRE, then you've probably accumulated a nest egg from years of work-oriented savings programs, such as a 401(k) or a Keogh. But what about money you saved on your own? It's time to take a look at all these various personal accounts and decide which ones you want to keep once you're retired. Here's a rundown on those accounts and their pros and cons, as well as their tax implications.

BANK CHECKING/SAVINGS/MONEY MARKET ACCOUNTS Checking accounts are handy for check-writing, debit cards, ATM machines, and teller access. Savings and money market accounts earn interest on short-term savings. *Pro:* Accounts offered by banks and savings and loans are all federally insured. (A money market account from a brokerage house is not usually federally insured.) *Con:* Any interest they pay won't keep up with the average annual rate of inflation, and they charge various service fees that can add up. *Taxes:* Any interest these accounts earn is taxed at your ordinary income tax rate.

CERTIFICATES OF DEPOSIT (CDs) These are contracts a bank makes with you to pay interest for the use of your money over a period of time, say three months to several years. *Pro:* They're federally insured. *Con:* Early withdrawals incur a penalty, and interest may just barely cover inflation (averaging 3.3 % over the past 80 years). *Taxes:* Although you don't actually receive any interest until the term ends, you do pay income tax out of your own pocket at the end of each year on that portion of the interest earned during the year.

MONEY MARKET MUTUAL FUNDS These short term savings accounts are available from mutual fund companies. *Pro:* They pay higher interest than bank accounts and CDs, plus you can write a few checks per month on them. *Con:* They aren't insured, and the minimum investment may be higher than the investment a bank would require. *Taxes:* Like other dividends, income is taxed at ordinary income tax rates during the year it is earned.

STOCKS These investments buy ownership in publicly-traded companies. *Pro:* As a company becomes more profitable, their stock price usually rises. The company may pay dividends, too. *Con:* Stock prices go down as well as up, and dividends aren't guaranteed. *Taxes:* Stock investments cause tax hits in two ways. First, since dividends are quarterly or annual payments, they get taxed just like interest—at ordinary income tax rates. Second, when you sell stock and its value has gone up, you pay taxes on the increase, called a *capital gains tax.* Alternatively, if the stock's value declines between the time you buy and sell, you'll get a tax deduction for the loss, called a *capital loss.*

BONDS These are contracts companies or governments make with you to pay interest for the use of your money over a period of time, usually a number of years. *Pro:* Bond prices tend to be more stable than stock prices, and interest is often higher than stock dividends. *Con:* Prices seldom appreciate as much as stocks. *Taxes:* Bonds pay interest that's taxed as income, just like the interest on your bank accounts. There are, however, a few twists. For example, interest on tax-free municipal bonds is not taxed federally, and some bonds are also free from state and/or local taxes.

MUTUAL FUNDS You buy shares in an account that pools your money with money from other investors to buy a variety of stocks and/or bonds. *Pro:* A professional picks investments on your behalf, for relatively little cost. *Con:* Performance and fees vary widely from fund to fund. *Taxes:* Most mutual funds pay dividends. Like other dividends, they're taxed at ordinary income tax rates during the year they are earned. You will be responsible for the taxes on the gains regardless of whether you reinvest or not. If you sell your shares in a fund, capital gains rules apply, as if it were a stock.

CAPITAL GAINS AND LOSSES

Capital—it's an old-fashioned word for invested money. A capital gain is the money you earn on investments, while a capital loss is the money you lose. Uncle Sam wants a piece of whatever you earn, but at a lower tax rate than ordinary income tax. If it's a *short-term gain* (money made on an investment held less than one year) you will be taxed at your ordinary tax rate. If it's a *long-term gain* (money made on an investment held more than one year) you will be taxed 20% if you are in the 28% bracket or higher. (If you are in a lower tax bracket, your tax is 10%.) If your investments go sour, you can deduct the loss against any capital gains and up to $3,000 per year against any other income.

IRAs

Investments that give you a tax advantage

THINK OF YOUR IRA AS A CONTAINER that can hold stocks, bonds, mutual funds, CDs, and other investments. What's unique about IRAs is that they let you defer paying taxes on those investments until you reach retirement age, which in IRA-land is 59½. The idea is that by that age your income will be less and you will be in a lower tax bracket than in your prime working years. Ergo, the taxes you now have to pay on your IRA investments will be less.

The U.S. government set up different types of IRAs to allow people to save for retirement. Chances are you have one or two IRAs lying around. Now it's time to sort through the paperwork and figure out what you've got.

INDIVIDUAL RETIREMENT ACCOUNTS (IRAs) Up until your retirement, you've probably been putting money into an IRA. If you earned less than $42,000 a year while single or $62,000 while married, then you had a **DEDUCTIBLE IRA.** This means that you were allowed to contribute up to $2,000 per year and deduct that contribution from your income. Now, when you are ready to withdraw, you will pay taxes on what you contributed as well as what you earned, presumably at a lower tax rate.

If you made more than that, you could still have contributed to an IRA, but the money you contributed would not have been tax-deductible. Hence its name—**NONDEDUCTIBLE IRA.** That said, all the money your investment earned got to grow, tax-free. So when you are ready to withdraw your money, you pay taxes only on what you earned, not what you contributed.

ROTH IRAS This type of IRA allows people who earned up to $110,000 if single, $160,000 if married to contribute up to $2,000 a year after taxes to a Roth IRA. The really good news is that "qualified withdrawals" from your Roth IRA earned are tax free as long as your account has been open for at least five years.

ASK THE EXPERTS

How do I know whether my IRA is a traditional deductible or a nondeductible IRA?

You were allowed to contribute to two kinds of IRAs. In the first kind, the annual contributions would appear on your old tax returns as deductions. In the second type of IRA account, the contributions consisted of money you had paid income tax on. Any of these contributions should have appeared on form 8606 of your tax return for the year you contributed. It's important to dig out this information—since you won't have to pay taxes again on that money when you withdraw it, only on the earnings from it.

Aren't there sometimes penalties on withdrawals from IRAs?

Yes. If you're under $59\frac{1}{2}$, you'll owe an additional 10% penalty on the amount withdrawn, as well as the regular income taxes—unless you become disabled. Then you pay only the ordinary income tax. You may also be able to get an exemption from the penalty for medical expenses that are above 7.5% of your gross income, payment of health insurance premiums if you are unemployed, and certain first-time homebuyer expenses. Talk to your accountant about how to proceed.

IRAs:
distributions and taxes

Once begun, annual distribution must continue

OH, HAPPY DAY, YOU FINALLY get to start withdrawing money from your IRA just like you planned. The IRS lets you start taking money out of your IRAs once you reach 59½. If you prefer, you can wait until you are 70½ before you withdraw a dime. These withdrawals are called **required minimum distributions** or **RMDs**. But watch out: If you don't start taking distributions by then, the penalty for "excess accumulation" is—take a deep breath—50% of the amount you should have taken. Clearly, the government wants you to withdraw all of the money from your IRA during your lifetime—and pay tax on income that was deferred, or face serious consequences.

In most cases, the money you put into the account was never taxed. And over the years, your IRA investments have been earning interest, dividends, and capital gains that were also never taxed. Now it's time to pay up. The good news is that since you are no longer working, you will probably be in a lower income tax bracket and so will pay less money in taxes on your IRA withdrawals.

Once you turn 70½, how do you know how much to withdraw each year? The amount you're required to take out is determined by a formula: Every year you look at your IRA's ending balance from the prior year and divide it by a factor based on the average life expectancy of a person your age, and your beneficiary's age, which the IRS has figured out for you. Look in the *Uniform Distribution Period* table, found in IRS Publication 590. (Get a copy of it by calling 800-829-3676, or download it from **www.irs.gov.** It's a good idea to check since the tables are periodically updated.) The amount of taxes you pay on your RMD will depend on two factors: your tax bracket and whether your IRA was deductible or nondeductible.

ASK THE EXPERTS

How do I go about beginning the withdrawal process for my IRAs?

If you have reached the magic age of 59 ½ , you can begin withdrawing money from your IRA. To do this, simply contact the bank, mutual fund company, or brokerage house that holds your IRA account. If you are 70 ½ , you must start this process or face stiff penalties.

If I have more than one IRA, do I have to take distributions from each?

You should calculate your RMD for each IRA separately. However, the IRS lets you add up all of your RMDs and take the total from one or more IRA(s) of your choice, as long as the total amount withdrawn is correct.

What happens to my IRA if I die before the age of 59 ½ ?

Funds in the IRA pass to your heirs without the penalty. However, they will have to pay income tax on the distribution. Whether estate taxes are owed depends on the size of your whole estate (see page 170).

FIRST PERSON DISASTER STORY

Beneficiary Blues

My dad's IRA was in the same bank where he had been a customer for 50 years. When he died after taking minimum distributions for ten years, his accountant told me that there was more than $100,000 left in the IRA, and that I was probably the beneficiary. When I called the bank, they said there was no beneficiary form on file for Dad's account. It must have gotten lost over the years. My accountant says that many institutions lose these forms, especially if there have been mergers or if the institution is too small to have a separate pension department. Since there is no beneficiary, the IRA becomes part of Dad's estate and all the money from the IRA has to be paid out and taxed over the next five years. Had Dad given me a copy of his IRA beneficiary form when he filled it out, I could have delayed the bulk of the taxes until I retired.

—Sherry Z., Abilene, Texas

Roth IRAs

It offers unique investment advantages if you plan to continue working

IN 1997 A NEW KIND OF IRA WAS BORN: the Roth IRA. Although you don't get a tax deduction on your contribution, it was an instant hit, because it has some advantages that are especially suitable to retirees:

- Income and capital gains earned are not just tax deferred, they're tax free. In other words, the Roth allows its owner to avoid taxes on whatever he earns. (Regular IRAs start taxing you when you take out money.)

- Uncle Sam doesn't make you take out Roth money if you don't need to, so it can continue to grow tax free. (The feds require annual minimum distributions from regular IRAs.)

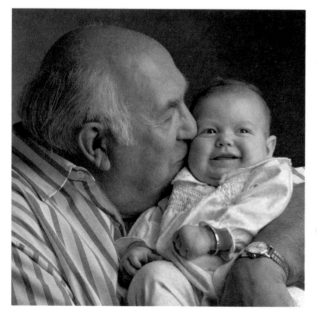

- Allowances for distributions before you turn 59½ are more lenient for Roths than for regular IRAs. For example, if you're a first-time home buyer, you can take out money tax free, as long as your Roth is at least five years old. If you need money for certain college or medical costs before you turn 59 ½ , you can withdraw Roth earnings penalty free, but you'll owe taxes on the earnings.

- As long as you're still working and have earned income, you can still contribute to a Roth account, regardless of your age. (You can't contribute to a regular IRA after you turn 70½ .)

The bottom line? If you have a Roth IRA, you'll want to spend it last, since 1) it continues to earn tax-free money; 2) it has few distribution restrictions; and 3) it can be left to you heirs.

ASK THE EXPERTS

When can I start taking distributions of earnings from my Roth IRA?

When you turn 59½ , as long as you've met the five-year "holding period requirement," you can take out as much as you want, tax free. (The clock starts once you make your first Roth IRA contribution.) But if you need the money before five years has passed, you'll generally owe tax on any withdrawals beyond your contributions.

If I'm taking minimum distributions from my regular IRA, but don't need the money, can I contribute them to my Roth IRA?

No. You can only contribute income you've earned from work.

I understand that I can "convert" my regular IRA to a Roth IRA. How?

You may convert part or all of your regular IRA to a Roth as long as your modified adjusted gross income is less than $100,000, excluding the amount of the Roth conversion. When you do this, you're essentially taking money out of your regular IRA, getting taxed on it, and then putting it into a Roth. While you would owe taxes now (on the amount converted), your future earnings and distributions would be tax free as long as you hold the part you converted for at least five years.

Is converting to a Roth IRA and paying the taxes on the amount converted a good idea when I am retiring?

Every situation is different; check with a professional adviser before making this decision. If you need to spend your IRA during retirement, then you won't mind taking the required minimum distributions of a regular IRA. Tax rates need to be considered, too. For example, if you're in a high tax bracket just before you retire but will be in a lower one after you retire, converting before you retire would mean that the amount you convert is taxed at higher rate, so you might wait. But a Roth conversion might be smart if you won't need the funds during retirement. Since there is no minimum distribution you have to take from a Roth, the money will grow, tax free, during your lifetime; then it'll pass to your heirs.

annuities

Reliable income is the prime attraction

WHAT IS AN ANNUITY? Well, it's a cross between an IRA and a life insurance policy. Like IRAs, annuities allow you to invest in a variety of assets (stocks, bonds, mutual funds), and the earnings on those investments are tax deferred. And just like IRAs, you can start to take your annuity payments as early as age 59½ , but like life insurance, there's no limit on the amount of annuity you can buy, and payments you receive are linked to actuarial tables.

During their working years, most people buy either a **Single Premium Deferred Annuity** or a **Variable Annuity.** Single Premium Annuities pay a fixed rate of return on the money you deposit. Variable Annuities are a little spicier since they are invested in one or more mutual funds and pay a potentially higher rate of return, but can also be more volatile.

Now that you are retiring, you may want to consider an **Immediate Annuity.** Here you buy an immediate annuity in one lump sum and then decide to take payments over a fixed period of time or over your lifetime. If you choose the lifetime payment option, your monthly payment will depend on your current age, your sex, and whether or not payments will continue to be paid to your spouse or the beneficiary when you die.

ASK THE EXPERTS

I'm scared that I'll run out of money. Should I buy an immediate annuity to make sure I'll receive payments for life?

It depends. The amount that the insurance company pays you is based on the assumption that you'll live to a certain age. If you die before that time, the insurance company will get to keep the rest of the payments. On the other hand, if you're healthy and have a family history of longevity, an immediate annuity might pay off for you. You could have a chance of outliving the insurance company's projection and coming out with even more payments than they had planned to give you.

My financial adviser is trying to talk me out of buying an annuity. He says bonds would be better. Why is that?

Most studies comparing annuities with other investments show that returns on annuities usually fall short after expenses and taxes are taken out. Remember, you pay 20% tax on a capital gain. So unless you're in a very high tax bracket and money has been socked away in the annuity for a long time, an annuity may not be a good idea. It's true, immediate annuities can give you peace of mind by providing guaranteed income each month. However, the high costs and low payouts make comparison shopping essential. For a steady rate of return you may find you'd be better off investing in bonds or other fixed-income assets instead.

I bought a variable annuity 15 years ago, and now I want to tap into it. How do I do that?

You have several choices. Choosing to "annuitize" essentially converts your variable annuity into an immediate annuity. While lifetime income is good in theory, few people actually make this choice. Why? The amount paid out is usually small, and the payments end with your death—even if the payments just began! If you want a continuous stream of income, consider going with fixed payments. And if you just need a one-time withdrawal, lump-sum options are available. If you die while you're taking fixed payments or a lump-sum payments, your beneficiaries are still entitled to receive any original contributions that haven't been taken.

now what do I do?

Answers to common questions

I'm trying to decide whether to tap into my IRA or my other investments to cover some living expenses. Any suggestions?

It depends on your tax situation and the size of your nest egg. Withdrawing from your non-IRA assets first is usually best. This is especially true if you're in a high tax bracket, since part of your withdrawals from non-IRA assets may be taxed at the lower capital gains rates instead of ordinary tax rates. If, however, you're in a low income tax bracket and you have a large IRA, you might want to start withdrawing money from your IRA before you need it. Why? As long as your withdrawals don't put you into a higher income tax bracket, you'll be able to draw down this account with low tax consequences. Finally, if you have a Roth IRA, this should be tapped last. If this sounds confusing, ask your tax adviser to help you understand the pros and cons of each choice.

I've always had a rainy day fund. Where should I invest it now that savings account rates seem so low.

Money Market Mutual Funds, described on page 126, are the ideal investment for boosting your returns without significantly increasing your risk. These funds are available from your favorite mutual fund company, and they generally allow you to write a few checks a month, should you need this money.

I hear tax-free bonds are a good investment. Would they be right for my IRA?

No, tax-free bonds have no place in an IRA or a Roth IRA. Retirement plans such as these are already tax deferred or tax free, so a tax-free bond would give you no advantage whatsoever. The same is true even in your regular portfolio if you're not in a high income tax bracket. The taxes you save must be sizable enough to make up for the lower rate of return that a tax-free bond pays.

I'm thinking about shifting all of my investments from stocks to bonds in order to generate more cash each month. Is this a good idea?

Not if you want your retirement money to last for a long time. While a total shift to bonds will boost your current income, over time inflation will eat away at your portfolio, and you'll be forced to deplete your savings. Instead, don't be afraid to maintain some stock exposure to offset inflation.

Aren't there sometimes penalties on early withdrawals from IRAs?

Yes. If you're under 59½ and withdraw any money, you'll owe a 10% penalty on the amount withdrawn, as well as the regular income taxes. If you become disabled and withdraw the money, you pay only the ordinary income tax. You may also be able to get an exemption from the penalty for medical expenses that are above 7.5% of your adjusted gross income, or if you're unemployed and you need the money to pay health insurance premiums.

NOW WHERE DO I GO?!

CONTACTS	BOOKS
www.invest-faq.com Comprehensive, unbiased introduction and reference to investing.	**You're Fifty—Now What?: Investing for the Second Half of Your Life** by Charles P. Schwab
www.troweprice.com **www.vanguard.com** These mutual fund companies provide a wide range of educational services on their sites.	**The Complete Idiot's Guide to Buying Insurance and Annuities** by Brian H. Brevel
www.IRAJunction.com An information source for investors with Individual Retirement Accounts.	**Financial Fitness for Life** by Jerry Mason

insurance needs

Life insurance 140
Is it time to cut back on this expense?

Medicare 142
It doesn't cover everything

Medigap insurance policies 144
Taking the sting out of Medicare limitations

Different types of healthcare plans . . . 146
HMOs, PPOs, fee for service—all have their
advantages

Paying for health insurance 148
What's out there if you're under age 65

Long-term care insurance 150
Almost half of those over 65 will need it

Buying long-term care insurance 152
Peace of mind can be expensive if you didn't buy
it at a young age

Medicaid 154
When your assets are all spent, this is your last
resort

Now what do I do? 156
Answers to common questions

Are long-term care insurance premiums tax deductible?

life insurance

You may not need this coverage anymore

BY NOW, YOU MUST KNOW THIS BIT of financial advice by heart: Life insurance buys you peace of mind because your loved ones are protected financially when you die. But along comes retirement, and guess what? Your situation may not require as much life insurance as when you were working. After all, it's likely that you no longer have to protect your dependents (they're out on their own), or your spouse (the mortgage may be paid for and childcare is just a memory).

If no one is relying on you for financial support anymore, it's time to check to see if other retirement income, such as your pension, will support your spouse after your death. Consider this:

- **IF YOU HAVE WHOLE-LIFE OR "PERMANENT" INSURANCE:** First, decide if the money you are spending on **premiums** (the amount you pay each year for the insurance) could be invested more wisely. Find out how much money you'd get if you cashed out now; this is called **cash value**. It's based on the insurance company's investment of the premiums you've paid up to this point (less administrative costs and the cost of the insurance itself). Then look at the opposite page to evaluate how you might put that money to use.
- **IF YOU HAVE TERM INSURANCE:** Many people buy a policy with the term expiring at retirement age. If the term's not up on your policy, and you don't need the coverage anymore, you can just cancel it. (Unlike a whole-life policy, term insurance doesn't have a "cash value" that you can retrieve.) But if the premiums are relatively low (usually they're not), you may want to hold on to the policy.

- **IF YOU HAVE A GROUP LIFE POLICY AT WORK (USUALLY TERM LIFE):** Ask your employer what happens to that policy when you retire. In some cases, the insurance ends promptly; in others, it may be phased out over a period of years with the company paying part or all of the premiums. If it ends, and you need to extend your coverage for any reason, you may be able to convert your employer's group coverage to an individual policy at a reasonable cost.

ASK THE EXPERTS

I have a whole-life insurance policy with a face value of $100,000, and the cash value at present is $50,000; I'm 67 and just retired. All my financial ducks are in order, and I feel I don't need this insurance coverage anymore. What should I do?

If you need income for retirement, cash out the policy. Take the money, plus what you've been spending on premiums, and invest it (see page 140). If you won't need the income, spend that money on your grandchildren or a dream vacation.

What if I need to preserve coverage to care for my wife, who is 15 years my junior, but I want to lower or eliminate the need to pay premiums?

You have several options:

- You can change your whole-life policy to *extended term* insurance. This way you stop paying premiums and use the cash value that has already built up in the policy to buy a term policy (paid in full, so no premiums) with the same face value as the original whole-life policy. The difference: The extended term policy is only good for a limited number of years.

- You can change your whole-life policy to *lifetime term* insurance. Like the extended term, you stop paying premiums and use the cash value to buy a paid-up term policy. But instead of being a policy for a limited time period, it's for life. The difference? When you die, lifetime term will pay less than an extended term policy.

- You might be able to reduce the face value of the policy. (Not all insurers will do this, but it won't hurt to ask.) You'll still pay premiums, but they'll be half the original amount.

TAKE CARE OF THE LAST RITES

You and your spouse might want to buy two small lifetime term insurance policies, one for each of you, to cover your funeral expenses and the costs of settling your estates. The amount should be $5,000 to $10,000, depending on your area and the size of your estate; ask your lawyer how much would cover everything.

medicare

Medicare is low-cost health insurance for people over 65

WHEN YOU TURN 65, YOU'RE eligible for Medicare, the health insurance plan offered by the federal government. You pay no **premiums** (or fees) for part of this coverage (Part A), and you pay very low premiums for the rest of it (Part B). In 2001, Part B cost $50 per month.

About 39 million Americans are currently covered by Medicare. Unlike Medicaid (with which it is often confused), Medicare coverage is not based on need. That means it doesn't matter if you're rich or poor. You're eligible for Medicare if you are 65 and you and/or your spouse have paid Medicare taxes at work for at least 10 years. (You can find out for sure by calling the Social Security Administration, 800-772-1213.)

PART A is hospital insurance. If you go into the hospital, you pay a deductible (the bills you pay for before the insurance starts to pay anything) and a portion of the costs; Medicare picks up the rest:

DAYS IN HOSPITAL	YOU PAY
0-60	$792 worth of bills
61-90	$194 per day
91-150	$388 per day

Medicare also pays a portion of your outpatient bills and covers short-term home healthcare and hospice care.

PART B is medical insurance. After you pay a deductible ($100 in 2001), Medicare covers 80% of the amount designated as appropriate for most doctors' fees, and for medical equipment and supplies (wheelchairs, pacemakers, etc.), and other services such as mammograms and X-rays that Part A doesn't cover. A few selected costs are covered at 100%.

ASK THE EXPERTS

What health services are not covered by Medicare?
Some of the services and supplies that Medicare does not cover—
under Parts A or B—include the following:

- most prescription drugs
- routine physical exams
- dental care
- routine foot care, such as corn or callus removal
- custodial care, such as assistance with bathing, eating, and dressing

- eyeglasses
- hearing aids
- dentures
- orthopedic shoes
- healthcare received while traveling outside the U.S.

(See page 144 to learn how to get coverage for these conditions.)

What is meant by the term "Medicare + Choice"?
That term can be misleading. Medicare + Choice is just a name that
Congress used broadly, in 1997, to include all Medicare-related
options, such as managed care Medicare plans. The term doesn't
mean that the basic Medicare program has changed.

HOW DO I GET MEDICARE COVERAGE?

You're automatically enrolled in Medicare the month you turn 65 if you already get Social Security benefits. If you are close to age 65—and not getting Social Security—you can apply for both Medicare and Social Security at the same time. You will receive a packet in the mail containing your Medicare card and instruction booklets. There will also be some forms to sign and return by mail. When you sign the forms, you'll be asked if you want Part B, which is optional. If you opt for Part B, the premiums are usually deducted from your monthly Social Security checks. (If you don't want to start your Social Security at 65, you will get a monthly bill for Part B premiums instead.) If you have questions, call 800-772-1213.

medigap insurance policies

A medigap policy picks up the slack in the Medicare program

IF MEDICARE DOESN'T PAY FOR A DEDUCTIBLE or part of your doctor's fees or for prescription drugs or dental work or podiatrists, who does? Good question—you do. Fortunately, to offset such costs, you can buy a medigap policy. It's a supplemental insurance policy sold by private insurance companies. As its name implies, it fills the gaps for many services that aren't covered by Medicare.

There are ten standard medigap plans to choose from, starting with the most basic (and cheapest) plan, A, and ending with the most comprehensive plan, J. The letter designations are required by law so that retirees can easily compare and evaluate the policies. Each of the policies offers various additional benefits. Plans H, I, and J, for instance, cover prescription drugs. Not all plans are available in all states, but in Minnesota, Wisconsin, and Massachusetts, you'll have even more choices. (See opposite page for chart outlining benefits for each plan.)

When shopping for a medigap policy, consider the services you need and the price. Plans F and J generally cost less, for example, because they have a high deductible. (You'll have to pay $1,580 out of pocket per year before this plan kicks in a dime.) All standardized medigap plans are also sold as Medicare "Select" Plans, which usually cost less because you must use certain doctors and hospitals (except in an emergency).

WHO SELLS MEDIGAP MANAGED CARE PLANS?

Contact your state insurance commissioner or the state Department for Aging to find out which insurance companies sell them in your area.

Although the benefits offered are standardized according to the letter designation on each plan, the cost of premiums is not. Premiums for the same plan can vary from one insurer to the next. You will want to shop around for the features you need at the cost you can afford.

THE STANDARD MEDIGAP PLANS

All companies offering medigap insurance must offer Plan A, consisting of basic benefits (below). They may also choose to offer any (or all) of Plans B-J.

THE BASIC BENEFITS

HOSPITALIZATION: The plan pays coinsurance for hospital days covered by Medicare **Part A.**

MEDICAL EXPENSES: The plan pays coinsurance for Medicare Part B (generally 20% of Medicare-approved expenses) after the $100 deductible is met.

BLOOD: The plan pays for the first 3 pints of blood used each year.

Coverage in Each Type of Plan	A	B	C	D	E	F*	G	H	I	J*
Basic Benefits	✔	✔	✔	✔	✔	✔	✔	✔	✔	✔
Part A: Inpatient Hospital Deductible		✔	✔	✔	✔	✔	✔	✔	✔	✔
Part A: Skilled-Nursing Facility Coinsurance			✔	✔	✔	✔	✔	✔	✔	✔
Part B: Deductible			✔			✔				✔
Foreign Travel Emergency			✔	✔	✔	✔	✔	✔	✔	✔
At-Home Recovery				✔			✔		✔	✔
Part B: Excess Charges						100%	80%		100%	100%
Preventive Care					✔				✔	
Prescription Drugs								Basic Coverage ✔	Basic Coverage ✔	Extended Coverage ✔

*Plans F and J also have a high deductible option. If you choose this option, you must pay **$1,580** out of pocket per year before the plans pay anything. Insurance policies with a high deductible option generally cost less than those with lower deductibles. Your out-of-pocket costs for services may be higher.

different types of *healthcare* policies

Insurance for early retirees

IF YOU RETIRE EARLY AND ARE NOT OLD ENOUGH FOR MEDICARE, there are three basic types of health insurance to consider getting:

FEE-FOR-SERVICE PLAN Also known as a traditional indemnity plan, it offers the most flexibility. You choose your own doctors and hospitals, and you can visit a specialist without getting approval from your regular doctor. The premiums are the most expensive. Also, you may pay an annual deductible of $500 to $1,500 before the insurance company starts paying your bills, and they usually pay just 80% of the "reasonable and customary" (average) medical fees; you're expected to pay the remaining 20% of that average plus any overage between what the doctor charges and the average fee. You often must pay bills up front and wait to be reimbursed from your insurance provider.

PREFERRED-PROVIDER OR POINT-OF-SERVICE PLAN You choose your primary care physician from a list of doctors who have agreed to accept fees proposed by the insurance company. Your primary care physician often must approve any other healthcare you receive. This insurance policy costs less than fee-for-service, and the co-payments (fees you pay for medical services) are likely to be lower. Some plans provide options for seeing doctors or going to hospitals not listed in their plan if you pay a higher percentage of the fees.

HEALTH MAINTENANCE ORGANIZATION, OR HMO This plan assigns your care to a doctor within its group (often housed together in a clinic). All other healthcare is subject to that doctor's approval and is performed only by specialists and hospitals within, or designated by, the HMO. The fees you pay for medical services are nominal, but if you see physicians or seek hospital care outside the HMO, you'll pay the costs in full.

WHEN YOU DO TURN 65, MEDICARE OFFERS SIMILAR OPTIONS FOUND IN THE PRIVATE SECTOR:

"Managed Care" Medicare Plan

The basic Medicare plan is a traditional fee-for-service plan. You choose your doctor and hospital; Medicare pays for submitted bills. But in recent years, Medicare recipients have been able to join managed care plans such as preferred-provider plans and Health Maintenance Organizations (HMOs) just like other insured individuals. These plans may offer the same benefits that you receive under the original Medicare plan, plus coverage of some of the gaps in Medicare. You pay a monthly premium to the managed care plan, and sometimes you pay minimal co-payments for services. Before picking a managed care plan, however, be sure you understand exactly what is covered and what the costs are.

A Medicare "managed care" plan is not a medigap policy. Rather, it's a different way of delivering Medicare benefits, plus it also covers many Medicare gaps and some services Medicare does not cover at all. Generally, these managed care plans are cheaper than medigap plans (even the "Select" variety) and offer more choices. You can pick from an HMO with a point-of-service option or a preferred-provider option.

"Medicare Select" Plan

Medicare "Select" is an HMO-type of medigap plan available in some states. The insurer offers a choice of some of the standardized medigap coverages A through J—to be used in conjunction with your basic Medicare coverage. However, the "Select" policy generally costs less than other medigap policies because you must use specific hospitals and in some cases specific doctors to get full insurance benefits (except in an emergency).

paying for *health* insurance

Medical coverage from your former employer is best

IF YOU RETIRE EARLY, THAT'S ANY time before age 65, you won't yet be eligible for Medicare. You need to think about your health insurance: Who's going to provide it? How much will it cost? And how far ahead will you have to purchase a new plan to cover preexisting conditions—health problems that you've had for a while, such as asthma or diabetes? Don't worry. You have some options:

YOUR FORMER EMPLOYER'S HEALTH PLAN If your company offers continuing health coverage after early retirement, great; go for it. Check any changes in the coverage, though. For example, the deductible may change for retirees, or fewer services may be covered. You may pay a monthly premium (the fee for insurance coverage) that's higher than the premium you paid while working.

COBRA/HIPAA If your employer doesn't offer early retirement medical insurance, you can buy it under the Consolidated Omnibus Budget Reconciliation Act (COBRA). Thanks to this Federal law, you are guaranteed the right to buy 10 months' coverage—individual or family—through your former employer's group plan. Benefits must be identical, but you'll pay the full premium (and it's usually pretty hefty.) After 10 months, the insurance company is required by the federal Health Insurance Portability and Accountability Act (HIPAA) to extend your coverage, regardless of preexisting conditions, but they may raise the rate. COBRA coverage is often cheaper than buying an individual policy on your own, and the follow-on policy, while even more expensive, may be worth it until you're eligible for Medicare.

AN INDIVIDUAL POLICY It's often the most expensive option because premiums are based on your age and medical history. Ask about coverage for preexisting conditions. Some insurers wait up to a year before they pay bills related to these conditions (in which case you will need to overlap such a policy with your COBRA coverage—an added expense). A few companies won't cover services related to preexisting conditions at all; avoid them.

TOP SIX COBRA FACTS

- You're covered under this law if your company employs 20 or more workers and offers its employees group health insurance.
- Your spouse and dependent children are also eligible for COBRA, sometimes for as long as 3 years.
- COBRA does not apply to federal employees, some church-affiliated organizations, or companies that employ fewer than 20 workers. It is also not available in the District of Columbia.
- To be eligible, you must have been covered under a former employer's health plan.
- Individual health insurance policies that you buy yourself are not subject to COBRA law.
- You must be offered identical plans (medical, hospitalization, dental, vision), but you have the option of dropping noncore benefits (dental or vision) if you don't want to pay for those.

FIRST PERSON   DISASTER STORY

Worth the Money at Any Price

My husband and I had been planning his retirement for years. We were thrilled when Harry's company offered him an early retirement package at 62, except there were no medical benefits. "Don't worry, Ethel," he said. "We'll have Medicare at 65, and I'll buy a policy to tide us over till then." Well, after his COBRA coverage ran out, the cost of extending the policy was going to be really expensive. So we decided to go without insurance until Medicare kicked in. But within a year, Harry had a really bad bout of pneumonia. He managed to stay out of the hospital, but just barely. Now we're sweating it out, hoping we make it to 65 before either of us has a medical emergency. We should have bought that insurance when we could. You just can't take chances with your health.

—**Ethel S., Manchester, New Hampshire**

149

long-term care
insurance

The costs of long-term care can wipe out a lifetime of saving

WAIT, DON'T TURN THIS PAGE. This is really important. The need for long-term care is rising—especially since so many of us are living longer, thanks to those good doctors. But while the doctors are brilliant at dealing with many acute problems—a heart attack, surgery for a broken hip—they can't do much for chronic conditions that require long-term care, such as a stroke, Alzheimer's, or Parkinson's.

This type of care—dubbed **long-term care** by the insurance industry— ranges from the skilled nursing services that you'd receive at a nursing home to the custodial care you'd receive in your own home if you needed help with the "activities of daily living." The costs for such services can be steep. One year in a nursing home can range from $30,000 to $100,000, depending on the state you live in and the facility you go to. Bringing an aide into your home for three three-hour visits per week to assist with bathing and dressing can run about $1,000 a month or more, again depending on the area in which you live. Yet costs for such care on a long-term basis are not covered by traditional health insurance.

That's right: *not covered*. Not by Medicare. Not by medigap policies. (Medigap plans D, G, I, and J do contain an at-home recovery benefit, but it's only for short-term assistance). Long-term care is not even covered by private health insurance or your employer's health insurance, or by any of the traditional forms of insurance that you've always relied on.

Yet almost half of America's elderly citizens will spend time in some type of long-term care. To protect yourself, you need a separate, long-term care insurance policy. Offered by life insurance companies, these policies vary widely in terms of eligibility requirements, restrictions, costs, and benefits. (See page 152.)

I'm in good health. Why should I get long-term care insurance?

None of us think that we're going to be the ones to get sick—especially if we've always enjoyed fairly good health. But the odds of entering a nursing home—and staying for longer periods—increase with age. By the year 2005, it's estimated that 9 million men and women over the age of 65 will need long-term care. One study, in fact, shows that 40% of people aged 65 and older will enter a nursing home. About 10% of those folks will stay there five years or longer.

But doesn't Medicare cover nursing home care?

Medicare will cover just 100 days of nursing home care, and only when it follows a hospital stay. And that's it. If you must stay longer (the average stay is two years), you'll be expected to pay the bill yourself.

If I need long-term care and I don't have a long-term care policy, who will pay for this care?

You will, until your money runs out. Once you've exhausted every bit of your investments and savings and met federal poverty guidelines for income and assets, you will be eligible for Medicaid. (Your spouse would be able to retain your home and a very small income. See page 155 for details.) Medicaid will pay the nursing home expenses for you indefinitely, but the nursing home you are in must be one that accepts Medicaid patients.

buying
long-term care
insurance

It's not too late to buy this protection

GREAT. YOU ACTUALLY READ ABOUT long-term care insurance. Now, do you need to buy some? It's not necessarily for everyone. According to the National Association of Insurance Commissioners:

You should not buy long-term care insurance if:
- You have limited assets; for example, you don't own a home.
- You don't have heirs who you want to inherit your assets.
- Your income is very low, say from Social Security benefits or Supplemental Security Income (SSI), so that you often have trouble paying for basic needs, such as food, medicine, housing, or utilities.

You should consider buying long-term care insurance if:
- You have significant assets and income that you want to pass along to your spouse or heirs.
- You want to pay for your own care independent of Medicaid or support from others.
- You want to protect your spouse from a drop in income should you need long-term nursing home care.

Here's how the pricing works: Like most other types of insurance, the younger you are when you buy the policy, the cheaper your premiums will be. Prices for long-term care insurance climb sharply once you hit age 65. It would have cost about $650 per year if you had bought a policy at age 45 that pays $100 a day for three years' care. At 65, that same policy will cost you about $1,550 per year.

Obviously, a good time to buy a policy is when you're a bit younger, say between the ages of 50 and 55, before the prices skyrocket and/or your health declines. In addition to rising costs, the other problem with waiting to buy a long-term care policy, of course, is that minor health problems can develop and may require you to pay a higher premium. The good news is, the premiums on long-term care policies may be tax deductible; check with your accountant. Many insurance companies offer long-term care policies. Look for a company that has been providing long-term care coverage for at least 10 years.

FEATURES TO CHECK OUT IN A LONG-TERM CARE POLICY

Daily benefit A policy that pays $100 per day will cost less than a policy that pays $200 per day.

Deductible (elimination period) A policy that starts paying after 100 days will cost less than one that starts after 20 days.

Services covered Will the policy cover in-home care? Under what conditions? Find out what services are excluded.

Waiver of premium This feature lets you stop paying premiums while you are receiving benefits.

Inflation protection Your benefits may be adjusted for inflation, but your premium remains the same.

Renewability Most polices are guaranteed renewable. That means the insurer can't cancel your policy even if you develop a terminal illness. However, they may raise your premiums.

State of Residence Nursing home costs vary from state to state. Check with several nursing homes in your area and ask about their cost per day.

Where can I get long-term care insurance?

Contact the National Council on Aging at 202-479-1200 for more information on long-term care insurance. A number of life insurance companies offer it. Contact: John Hancock, **www.johnhancock.com**, 800-695-7389; Continental Casualty, **www.contwestins.com**, 800-235-CWIC; Fidelity National Financial, Inc., **www.fnf.com**, 888-934-3354; Mass Mutual, **www.massmutual.com**, 888-229-7540.

IF YOU'RE RESISTING

You're in good company. Because long-term care insurance is so expensive, many advisers counsel retirees who could afford three years in a home (about $100,000 in many states) not to buy it. Or they suggest that you simply invest the money you might pay for long-term care insurance in a special account. Chances are, by the time you need a nursing home, the account will be large enough to take care of the bills. And if you never need it, the money is available for your heirs. Granted, there's a risk, since you could get sick before the account is big enough to cover long-term care expenses. But that is a risk many people feel comfortable enough to take.

medicaid

MEDICAID. MEDICARE. THESE NAMES SOUND so much alike that it's no wonder people often confuse them. They are both national health insurance programs, but they are *not* interchangeable.

- Medicare is a health insurance program for people age 65 or older. (You may also qualify for Medicare if you're a younger person with a disability or with chronic kidney disease.)
- Medicaid is a health insurance program for low-income people of any age. You can be young, old, or in-between to qualify for Medicaid.

Only if your money runs out—all of it— will Medicaid pay your long-term care bills

Medicaid is a federal program, but it is administered by the states. That means the rules for eligibility and coverage can vary from one state to the next. State regulations even affect how you apply for Medicaid; in one state you go through your local county social services office, in another you go to the welfare office, and in another you must find the Department of Human Services office.

If you qualify for Medicaid and are over 65, it's possible that you'll receive coverage from both Medicare and Medicaid. Medicaid, for instance, can pay your Medicare deductible, your Medicare Part B premium, and that 20% of charges not paid by Medicare. In many states, Medicaid also covers services and costs that Medicare does not cover, such as prescription drugs, eyeglasses, and nursing home care, although you might have to pay a small amount for certain services.

SK THE EXPERTS

What long-term care services does Medicaid pay for?

It covers costs for an extended nursing home stay and/or assisted living at home. If you or your spouse need such care (called "custodial care," because it does not require major medical services), and you don't have long-term care insurance to cover the charges (see pages 150-152), you'll have to tap into your personal savings to pay the bills. Only when your money runs out does Medicaid kick in.

What is this "spend down" business all about?

To qualify for Medicaid as the insurance of "last resort," you must have spent everything you have. Whether you wind up on Medicaid or rely on it from the start, the drawback is the same: You must generally exhaust all of your assets and money before Medicaid will help you. The regulations shift slightly from time to time, but currently you must have no more than your home and furnishings, a car, a burial plot, and money for burial expenses to go on Medicaid, and your spouse also must have few assets and little income.

Are all nursing homes required to accept Medicaid?

The most desirable nursing homes often don't accept Medicaid patients at all, since Medicaid usually doesn't pay the full amount they charge. Some that have a few designated Medicaid beds will take you as a nursing home resident paying the full fees, then hope to switch you to a Medicaid bed when you run out of money. But if there is no Medicaid bed available at the time you need it, there is a slight chance that they might just ask you to leave. Transferring to a nursing home that accepts Medicaid can be a problem at that point. If nursing home care is recommended for you or your spouse, it is wise to get advice from a social worker or a lawyer who specializes in elder care in your area.

TRANSFERRING YOUR ASSETS

If you want to transfer your assets to your heirs, hoping to fall back on Medicaid if you should need long-term care, check out your plans with a lawyer specializing in elder care so you can avoid any difficulties. The feds are allowed to examine the last three years of your financial transactions at the time you apply for Medicaid. If a transfer was made to defraud the government and make it seem that you have no assets, you could be subjected to fines and even jail time.

now what do I do?
Answers to common questions

I'm thinking about tapping into my life insurance policy to have a little extra spending money. What are the financial consequences?

It depends. If you borrow against the policy, you'll be charged interest, and the amount your heirs receive will be reduced accordingly. If you cash in your policy, you'll get taxed on any earnings that might have built up while you owned it, and you'll reduce your coverage. See pages 140-141 for more on cashing in your life insurance.

What's not covered in a long-term care policy?

Limitations and exclusions will differ from policy to policy. But in general, long-term care policies often don't cover mental and nervous disorders such as depression and schizophrenia, alcoholism and drug abuse, and self-inflicted injuries. If, when you buy the plan, you have preexisting health problems that will lead to long-term care, such as Alzheimer's or Parkinson's disease, they won't be covered either.

Are long-term care policy premiums tax-deductible?

Yes, but it isn't simple. First, you must itemize deductions. Next, the amount you can deduct depends on your age, the top limit being $2,570 at age 70. Finally, you must add the premiums to your other medical premiums and expenses for the year and determine how much exceeds 7.5 % of your adjusted gross income. For example, if your adjusted gross income for the year is $50,000, you can only deduct medical expenses that exceed $3,750. If all your medical expenses and premiums for the year add up to $4,000, you will only be able to deduct $250.

I've heard that there's a financial advantage to buying medigap insurance soon after going onto Medicare. How does that work?

If you buy within six months of enrolling in Medicare Part B, you cannot be turned down or charged extra due to any preexisting health condition. After that, an insurance company can charge extra if you are in poor health or even refuse to sell you a policy. (Some states have different rules; check your state insurance agency.)

Do I need collision or comprehensive insurance on my old car?

No. If your car is at least five years old, an insurer won't pay much for it. You should only insure items that you can't afford to replace. (The same goes for extending appliance warranties.)

Now that I'm retired, do I still need disability insurance?

No. In fact, you can't buy such a policy even if you want it. Disability insurance replaces income, so you can't buy a policy unless you're earning a salary. (Investment income doesn't count.) Even if you're taking care of your wheelchair-bound spouse around the clock, you can't buy a disability policy unless you're receiving an income.

Is there a lot of paperwork involved in submitting Medicare claims?

Medical providers are required to submit your bills to Medicare for payment, so you do not have to bother with that paperwork. Once Medicare pays, the providers send you bills for the amount Medicare doesn't cover. It's a good idea to get a copy of all the bills your doctor is sending to Medicare.

NOW WHERE DO I GO?!

WEB ADDRESSES

www.insure.com
This consumer insurance site helps you research insurance issues and find answers to your insurance questions.

www.acli.org
Consumer-oriented site for the American Council of Life Insurance, a trade group. Helpful info on life insurance and long-term care insurance.

www.medicare.gov
or **800-633-4227**
This federal government site offers answers to frequently asked questions about Medicare, Medicaid, and Medigap policies. The site also has a link called "Medicare Compare" that connects you with Medicare managed care plans.

BOOKS

The Complete Idiot's Guide to Buying Insurance and Annuities
by Brian H. Brevel

Life and Health Insurance
by Kenneth Black
and Harold D. Skipper, Jr.

Medicare and You 2001
by the Health Care Financing Administration

CHAPTER TEN

Estate planning

Your estate 160
What happens to all your assets after you're gone?

Wills 162
Seeing that your wishes are carried out

The executor's job 164
Picking someone with time to give

Power of attorney 166
Decision-making while you're still here

Trusts 168
Avoiding probate

Tax consequences for your heirs 170
You may not have to worry

Funeral planning 172
Avoid what you don't want

Now what do I do? 174
Answers to common questions

I drafted a will about 15 years ago, so I'm all set, right?

your *estate*

Divvying up your stuff

MAYBE YOU THINK THAT ESTATE PLANNING IS for rich retired people. Perhaps you have a plan in place, but you haven't reviewed it lately. Now that you've retired, it's important to start thinking about how you want your property to be divided up after you're gone. You finally have time to review all your legal issues and create what estate planners call an "exit strategy." Your planning is sure to save your heirs money, time, and heartache.

The box below spells out different ways that your possessions pass to your heirs. An estate-planning attorney can be invaluable in helping you get the paperwork done.

RED FLAG

The biggest mistake people (even rich ones) make in estate planning is not realizing that joint tenancy and beneficiary designations on insurance and IRAs override any provisions in a will or a trust.

How asset is held	Examples	How it Works
Joint tenancy or Tenancy by the Entirety (a common way for married people to own property)	Houses, cars, checking accounts, investments, etc.	Assets pass directly to the other joint tenant at your death, regardless of what wills or trusts say.
Beneficiary Designations	Life insurance, 401(k) plans, IRAs	Assets pass directly to the named beneficiary at your death, regardless of what wills or trusts say.
Payable on Death (POD) Designations	Bank accounts, investment accounts	Assets pass directly to the named beneficiary at your death, regardless of what wills or trusts say.
Wills	Assets not held in joint tenancy and without a beneficiary, such as artwork, jewelry, computers	Assets pass to those named in your will, after proceeding through the court system in a process called "probate" (see page 162).
Intestate (no will or trust)	Same type of assets as those covered in wills, joint tenancy, or POD	Assets pass to heirs in the order designated by state laws. Requires court proceedings to determine proper heirs.
Trusts	Same type of assets as those covered in wills, joint tenancy, or POD	Assets pass to those named in your trust. No court probate process is required.

YOUR ESTATE

Use this chart to help you identify your assets and liabilities. Start by listing their approximate value. Date the list and put it in a fireproof box in your home. Tell your heirs where you keep it.

ASSETS	ACCOUNT NAME & NUMBER	APPROX. VALUE
Financial Assets		
Bank accounts	_____	_____
Stocks	_____	_____
Bonds	_____	_____
Mutual Funds	_____	_____
401(k)s	_____	_____
Individual Retirement Accounts (IRAs)	_____	_____
Annuities	_____	_____
Home	_____	_____
Other Real Estate	_____	_____
Life Insurance Death Benefit	_____	_____
Other Financial Assets	_____	_____
Other Assets		
Cars	_____	_____
Jewelry, Watches	_____	_____
Computer Equipment	_____	_____
Furniture	_____	_____
Antiques, Art, & Other Collectibles	_____	_____
Other Assets	_____	_____
TOTAL ASSETS:		
Less: Liabilities		
Mortgage	_____	_____
Credit Card Debt	_____	_____
Taxes	_____	_____
Auto Loans	_____	_____
Student Loans	_____	_____
Other Loans	_____	_____
TOTAL LIABILITIES:	_____	_____
NET ESTATE VALUE:	_____	_____
(TOTAL ASSETS MINUS TOTAL LIABILITIES)	_____	_____

wills

They help ensure that your wishes will be respected

AFTER YOU FIGURE OUT WHAT YOUR ASSETS are and where you want them to go, how do you make sure your bequests will happen? Drafting a **will** is the first step. A will specifies who gets your money and property after you die. It names a person to handle your affairs—known as the **executor**; and if you have any children who are minors or disabled, your will needs to name a **guardian** who will look out for their welfare in your stead.

What if you die without a will? It's known as dying **intestate**. When that happens, the government takes control of your estate and a court decides who gets your assets, based on the laws of the state where you live. This can be a long and very public process, and by the time your heirs see any money, a chunk of it is likely to have gone to the court-appointed lawyers.

You can make a will by yourself; legal kits, books, and software can give you instructions. But it is wise to have an estate-planning attorney review your work to help you avoid pitfalls such as willing property that is jointly owned (a common mistake).

No matter how you decide to spell out your last will and testament, nothing is engraved in stone while you are alive. So if circumstances change during your lifetime, you can modify your will at any time.

WHAT IS PROBATE?

The job of the probate court is to make sure your will has been signed and witnessed correctly, that all your taxes and debts have been paid, and that your documented wishes are carried out. Your executor oversees this public process, usually with an attorney's help. This can take anywhere from a few weeks to a year, depending on your estate's complexity (and the court's efficiency), and will incur court costs, filing fees, and recording fees. A trust (see page 168) allows you to bypass probate.

ASK THE EXPERTS

What's a living will?

It's a document explaining your general wishes about your own healthcare in case you are incapacitated and unable to make decisions for yourself (see Power of Attorney, page 166).

My spouse and I will leave our assets to each other, and then to our children. Will there be any estate taxes to pay?

It's important in drawing up your wills to work out how to minimize any tax bite that might diminish what you leave behind. No taxes are due when the first spouse dies, since you can pass unlimited assets to your spouse without any tax consequences. When your assets ultimately pass to your kids, however, they'll incur taxes if your estate exceeds certain levels. Estate taxes can usually be avoided by properly structuring your wills and trusts.

I hear that estate tax laws might be repealed. Shouldn't I wait until this is final before doing any planning?

Even though the laws regarding estate taxation are being repealed, you still need to plan your estate now. Saving estate taxes is just one part of estate planning.

FIRST PERSON   DISASTER STORY

When the Will Doesn't Count

I grew up in a beautiful home that I'd always dreamed of owning. I often talked to Mom and Dad about my desire to live there one day. After Mom died, Dad remarried, but he assured me that he had arranged for the home to eventually be mine. After his death, I was shocked to learn that his new wife was selling it. Turns out that although Dad did specify in his will that the house should go to me, he had retitled the home in joint tenancy with his wife. That meant that the will didn't apply, and the house passed to her.

— Sara E., Willow Springs, Illinois

the
executor's
job

Find someone who can afford the time

YOU'LL NEED TO DECIDE WHO WILL OVERSEE the transfer of your assets to your heirs. If you're married, you'll probably choose your spouse as your **executor**. But what if you're single? Or if you and your spouse die at the same time? Who should handle all of your affairs? If you choose one of your children, nieces, or nephews, who will you choose?

Before you decide on your executor, look at what the job entails. Talk to the person you choose as executor to make sure he or she feels equal to the task. Go over a copy of your will, so that you can answer any questions your executor might have.

The executor:
- Opens and inventories your safe-deposit box.
- Gets copies of your death certificate and distributes them to the insurance companies, banks, and other institutions where your assets are located.
- Files your will with probate court if necessary.
- Inventories all of your assets and insurance policies.
- Sells any assets and household goods that must be disposed of.
- Pays all of your debts and any income taxes owed the year you died.
- Keeps funeral expense records.
- Notifies the Social Security Administration of your death with a copy of the death certificate, and finds out if any survivor benefits are available.
- Hires any necessary professionals to help in the process of settling the estate: lawyers, accountants, or investment professionals.

● Gets the full names, addresses, and Social Security numbers of everyone named in the will or trust and distributes the inheritance according to the document's instructions.● Puts a death notice in the local newspaper.

ⒶSK THE EXPERTS

I drafted a will about 15 years ago, so I'm all set, right?

Not necessarily. Because of changes in your family status, financial situation, and estate-tax laws, your estate-planning documents should be reviewed every few years. Also, if you move out of state, your documents need to change to reflect the laws where you live.

What if I need to change my will after it's been drafted?

Changes to wills are called **codicils**. They are necessary for any major changes, such as the birth of another child or the sale of an important asset listed in the will. Codicils need to be written out, signed by you and two witnesses, and added to the will.

Can I avoid the probate process?

Yes. If you have an "I Love You" will giving all of your assets to your spouse, your estate probably won't need to go through probate or be required to pay any estate taxes (see page 170). Also, any assets that are in joint tenancy, or have a named beneficiary, or are "payable on death" will avoid probate since these assets pass directly to the heir without being subject to your will or probate. But the remaining spouse will not have the luxury of avoiding probate, so it might be a good idea for both husband and wife to set up living trusts (see page 168), not only to avoid probate but to keep the estate from being diminished by estate taxes when the second spouse dies.

CHECKLIST FOR CHOOSING AN EXECUTOR

● You trust the person.
● The person is geographically close to your assets and records.
● The person has time to devote to your estate.
● The person is capable of handling all the necessary tasks.

power of *attorney*

*If your affairs
need looking after
while you're alive*

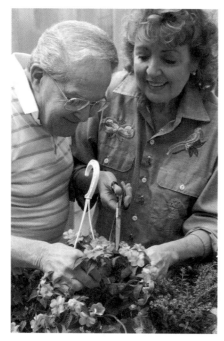

BY NOW YOU'VE PONDERED HOW THINGS might be handled when you go. But what happens if tragedy strikes and leaves you mentally or physically incapacitated? Who will make decisions on your behalf? More important, who will be recognized by the government, doctors, and the business world as empowered to make decisions for you?

By having a few simple documents on hand, you can solve this dilemma. The person you give **power of attorney** to will legally be able to look after your interests, should you become unable to do it for yourself. There are two basic types of power of attorney, one to cover your finances, another to cover your health. The documents vary from state to state, so be sure to discuss the details with an attorney. Here are the basics:

PROPERTY POWER OF ATTORNEY This document allows you to name someone, called your **agent,** to make financial decisions for you if you are unable to make them for yourself. This can either be effective immediately, or you can have it take effect once your doctor certifies that you're unable to give prompt and intelligent attention to your affairs. For example, if you were in a coma and your spouse needed to sell your jointly-held home, having a property power of attorney in place (with your spouse named as your agent) would allow him or her to sign on your behalf.

HEALTHCARE POWER OF ATTORNEY This document allows you to name someone, called your agent or representative, to make decisions on your behalf regarding your medical treatment. It also grants powers regarding autopsy and organ donation in the event of your death, and it allows you to document your feelings about life support and under what circumstances to pursue it.

ASK THE EXPERTS

What's the difference between a living will and a healthcare power of attorney? Do I need both?

A living will communicates the specific medical treatment you want (most often regarding the level of life support) should you become unable to discuss this with your doctor yourself. The power of attorney document names a person to make decisions on your behalf about any aspects of your healthcare not specified in the living will. Here's the catch: Even though living wills can be more difficult to make operative, they have precedence over the power of attorney. This is why some lawyers suggest having only a POA. That way your representative can make decisions in response to all situations that might arise, including your wishes about specific treatments such as extended life support.

What's an involuntary conservatorship?

If you have not signed a power of attorney document, a greedy relative or even a nursing home might convince a judge that you cannot care for yourself. If the judge awards an involuntary conservatorship to such an agent, you could lose the rights to your income, your assets, your car—and even your right to vote. But by having a power of attorney document, you can insure that someone you trust will be the only conservator of your affairs.

I am widowed. Who should I choose to act as my agent? A close relative? My executor?

It is a question of who might be attentive if you are sick, and whose judgment you can rely on. If you were to be sent to the hospital with a serious ailment, who would visit you most often there? Is that person someone you can trust to make major healthcare decisions for you? Your executor might be a good choice, provided he or she would be available if you are ill. If you happen to have a close friend who is a doctor or nurse, that person might also be a possible choice.

trusts

Legal arrangements to keep your assets out of probate court

A TRUST IS ANOTHER WAY OF OWNING your property and distributing it to your heirs. An especially nifty feature of trusts is that they allow your estate's assets to pass directly to your heirs—without subjecting them to the time and expense of the probate process (see page 162).

LIVING TRUSTS are the most common type of trust—they can act as a will substitute. A living trust costs more for your attorney to create than a will, but if it keeps your estate from being dragged through the probate court, it could be money well spent.

If you have a significant estate (more than $1,350,000), some trusts, like credit shelter trusts (see page 171), irrevocable life insurance trusts, and charitable trusts, can actually save you estate taxes.

There are generally three parties to a trust:

THE GRANTOR: The person who gives the assets to the trust.

THE TRUSTEE: The person who makes sure that the trust's instructions are followed.

THE BENEFICIARY/IES: Those who receive the assets from the trust.

If you create a living trust, you are the grantor, the trustee, *and* the beneficiary while you're still alive. At your death, the trustee you named as successor will take over implementing the trust, and the trust's assets will pass to your beneficiaries according to your wishes.

	WILLS	LIVING TRUSTS
WHO ARE THE PARTIES INVOLVED?	Testator—You, the person who makes the will. Executor—A person who administers the will after your death.	Grantor—You, the person who transfers property. Trustee—A person who legally owns the property once the grantor has transferred property title to the trust. (With a living trust, this can also be you.) Beneficiary—A person who inherits the assets from the trust.
WHEN DOES THE DOCUMENT TAKE EFFECT?	Once you sign the will before witnesses, it is legal, but it doesn't take effect until you die.	Once a living trust is signed, and you transfer assets to the trust, it is in effect.
WHAT HAPPENS WHEN YOU DIE?	The will becomes irrevocable, and the executor carries out its provisions. The will must go through the probate process, which the public has access to, and which can be costly and time-consuming. (Probate may be bypassed if all of the assets pass to the spouse.)	The revocable trust becomes irrevocable, and the trustee you designated carries out its provisions privately, without court supervision.
WHAT IF YOU BECOME INCAPACITATED DURING YOUR LIFETIME?	Since it doesn't become effective until after your death, the will can't be used to indicate your preferences should you become incapacitated.	A living trust can designate how your affairs should be handled in the event of incapacity.

tax
consequences for your heirs

Plan ahead, and the government won't take as much

ON TOP OF ALL THE PROFESSIONAL FEES, court costs, and other expenses you might get hit with, your beneficiaries might have to pay estate taxes. As of 2001, if the total value of your estate (financial assets as well as the appraised value of your home, cars, art, jewelry, etc.) is less than $675,000, relax: estate taxes probably won't apply to you. If it's more than $675,000—and you're concerned about minimizing the estate's tax liability—keep reading. (In 2002, the number rises to $1,000,000.)

With estate tax rates starting at 37% and quickly climbing to 55%, these taxes can take a huge bite out of assets you leave to your loved ones—but only the amount exceeding the $675,000 cutoff.

Here's what you need to know:

- Any and all assets you leave to a spouse or a charity are not subject to estate taxes.

- Once you deduct assets left to a spouse or a charity, only the portion of your remaining assets that exceed the $675,000 limit are subject to estate tax.

- If you're married and both your estates are structured properly, you can potentially leave a combined $1,350,000 ($2,000,000 in 2002 and 2003) to your children without paying estate taxes.

- Say you leave 100% of your property to a spouse. Sure, no estate taxes are taken out, but you've lost a chance to leave $675,000 worth of tax free assets to heirs other than your spouse. The result? When your spouse dies, only the portion of your joint estate covered by your spouse's exclusion of $675,000 will pass tax free to heirs. If you, too, had left up to $675,000 worth to heirs other than your spouse, you could have used the full $1,350,000 exclusion allowed for a married couple.

OPTIONS FOR MINIMIZING TAXES

If your estate is large enough for estate taxes to be a concern, talk to an estate-planning attorney about whether any of these techniques might benefit your heirs.

Gifts: If you're leaving money to family and friends, consider giving them part of their inheritance while you're still alive. (They don't pay income tax on these gifts, but you do if it's over a certain amount.) Giving money away helps to deplete your estate, not to mention provide you with the chance to see your loved ones enjoy the money. Uncle Sam lets you give away up to $10,000 per person per year, without any tax consequences (estate or personal) to you or to them. If you give more than that, you'll need to file a gift tax return (see box).

Charitable Donations: Consider leaving at least a portion of your estate to your favorite charity. Assets left to a charity escape any and all taxes. In fact, if you set up a trust for a charity during your lifetime, you'll get an income tax deduction at that time. Better still, you can receive income from the trust as long as you live. At your death the money would pass—estate-tax free—to the charity.

Credit Shelter Trust: If the estate you and your spouse will leave behind is at least $1.4 million, you might want to set up a **Credit Shelter Trust** (also known as a Bypass Trust or an A-B Trust). This allows $675,000 of a couple's estate to go into a trust for the children (or other heirs) when the first spouse dies. All assets exceeding the $675,000 flow to the surviving spouse, who can also use any income generated by the trust. When the surviving spouse dies, the second $675,000 exclusion is applied to the remaining estate. But before setting up this trust, you must be sure that your spouse won't need the first $675,000 principal that will be shielded in the trust.

GIVING MORE THAN $10,000

You can give your assets away in any amounts you wish, whenever you wish. However, if you give more than $10,000 in any year to a single recipient, be sure to file IRS form 709. This tax return tracks your gifts and calculates the tax you owe if you give away more than allowed each year.

funeral planning

Work out the details in advance

IT'S UNCOMFORTABLE TO THINK ABOUT your own death and the arrangements your family would have to make for you. But, because such choices are rarely discussed beforehand, your survivors are left to make costly decisions when they are least able to think straight. Fortunately, prearranged funerals seem to be on the upswing. With a little advance planning on your part, family and friends will be relieved of the important decisions and feel secure that they're doing what you would have wanted.

There are two ways you can help prearrange your funeral:

● Preplan. By doing your funeral and burial homework in advance, you can lay out your preferences ahead of time. Here are the main choices to consider: Do you want to be buried or cremated? Do you want a simple or top-of-the-line casket? Which cemetery do you prefer? Documenting the products and services that you want and discussing them with your family ahead of time will help them during a very stressful time. Some folks even set up a bank account earmarked for these future expenses.

● Prepay. This takes preplanning a step further by contracting with a funeral home, cemetery, and/or casket dealer, and providing payment in advance. In order for people to feel comfortable with this arrangement, most contracts can be funded with a trust, annuity, or burial insurance policy to ensure that the money will be available when needed. If you go this route, make sure you understand how the arrangement is funded, and then let your loved ones know. Also, carefully review any cancellation policies, in case you change your mind later on.

Give instructions to your family so they can access the policy, receipts, and plans you have made when needed. By the way, your safe-deposit box is not a good place to keep such information because it might be sealed for weeks in the event of your death (unless the box is held jointly). A fireproof box or file at home would be more convenient.

ASK THE EXPERTS

What does a funeral entail and how much does it cost?

A funeral home provides a variety of goods and services, including planning assistance, care of the body, transporting it to and from the funeral home, and use of the funeral home and equipment for wakes, visitation, and even the funeral itself. The industry average for these goods and services (including a casket) is about $5,000. Note: Caskets can be the most expensive part of a funeral. Caskets are made from a wide variety of wood or metals and lined with either velvet or crepe. Prices range from $600 or so for a simple pine box to elaborate tombs exceeding $7,000. Additional items to consider include fees for the clergy, organist and other musicians, obituary fees, cost of flowers and thank-you notes, and limo transportation for the family. These can add up to $1,000 to the cost of a funeral.

I heard that burial vaults are more expensive than grave liners. What's the difference?

Grave liners are required by most cemeteries to keep the ground from settling over time. Burial vaults serve the same purpose, but are made of concrete or other solid materials so they also protect the casket. These can range anywhere from $500 to $2,000 or more.

How can I get costs up front from the local funeral homes?

The FTC requires funeral homes to provide general price lists (by telephone or in person) for each product and service they provide. Call several local funeral homes and get their price lists so you can compare costs.

now what do I do?

Answers to common questions

How do I choose an attorney to help me plan my estate?

Start by getting names of estate-planning attorneys from friends and family. Interview likely candidates, asking about the process that would be used to prepare your estate and the fees involved. Find out about the attorney's background, education, experience, and areas of specialization. Does he or she work with many clients whose demographics are similar to yours? And whose estate size is similar to yours? Finally, assess how you feel when talking with this attorney. Do you feel comfortable or talked down to?

I have shares of Sears stock my granddad bought for me when I was born. They're now worth over $100,000. What are the most efficient ways to leave the stock to a charity or to my heirs?

Whatever you do, don't sell the shares to give the proceeds away. That would subject you to capital gains tax on the difference between the purchase price and the sale price. For estate-planning purposes, here are two alternatives. First, consider giving the shares themselves to a charity. By donating the shares, 1) you get an income tax deduction for the shares' current value; 2) you don't pay capital gains tax on the gain; and 3) the charity can sell the shares without tax consequences. Or, if you will the stock to your heirs when you die, they could sell it immediately and pay no capital gains tax. Heirs are "assumed" to have bought the stock on the day you died for its current price. The "assumed" price equals the sales price, so no tax would be due. But if you give it to your heirs before you die, and they sell it immediately, they would pay capital gains tax because the "assumed" price is what the price was when you bought it.

This is my second marriage, so I'm concerned about providing for my children from my first marriage.

Your attorney might recommend a Qualified Terminable Interest Property trust (also known as a Q-TIP). This trust allows you to pass property to your spouse when you die—but requires the property to pass to your children after your spouse dies.

What are estate taxes and aren't they being repealed?

Unlike income or Social Security taxes, which hit as income is earned, estate taxes are a one-time slap on the value of your assets when you die. What assets? Basically, all your money and the appraised value of your goods. With rates starting at 37%, these taxes can take a huge bite out of the money you leave to your loved ones. While legislation has been passed recently to gradually phase out the estate tax, current laws are scheduled to "sunset" on December 31, 2010. This means that if both branches of Congress and the president don't agree on a new bill, estate tax laws will revert to their 2001 rate specifications.

What should I look for in a funeral parlor?

First of all, consider a funeral parlor whose location is convenient to the family members. You should also consider the home's reputation for service, and any personal experience you've had at other people's funerals. Given the high cost of funerals, the fees must be considered, too.

NOW WHERE DO I GO?!

CONTACTS

www.nolo.com/encyclopedia/ret_ency.html
Look for user-friendly articles on a variety of estate planning topics.

www.smartmoney.com/estate

www.estateweb.com

National Network of Estate Planning Attorneys
One Valmont Plaza
Fourth Floor
Omaha, NB 68154
Tel: 303-446-6100
Fax: 303-446-6060
www.netplanning.com/consumer

American Academy of Estate Planning
9360 Towne Centre Drive
Suite 300
San Diego, CA 92121
Tel: 800-846-1555
www.aaepa.com

National Association of Financial & Estate Planning
525 E. 4500 South, F-100
Salt Lake City, UT 84107
Tel: 801-266-9900
Fax: 801-266-1019
www.nafep.com

International Cemetery and Funeral Association
1895 Preston White Drive
Reston, VA 20191
800-645-7700
www.icfa.org

BOOKS

Wealth: Enhancement & Preservation
by Robert A. Esperti and Renno L. Peterson.

Caring for the Dead: Your Final Act of Love
by Lisa Carlson

longevity basics

Healthy living **178**
Seven things you need to know

Eating right **180**
Now's the time to get with the program

Exercise **182**
It can really improve your life

Recommended checkups **184**
Fix little stuff before it gets to be big stuff

Memory loss **186**
It's not usually as bad as the jokes you hear about it

Grief **188**
Coping with loss of a loved one

Depression **190**
Sadness can get serious

Now what do I do? **192**
Answers to common questions

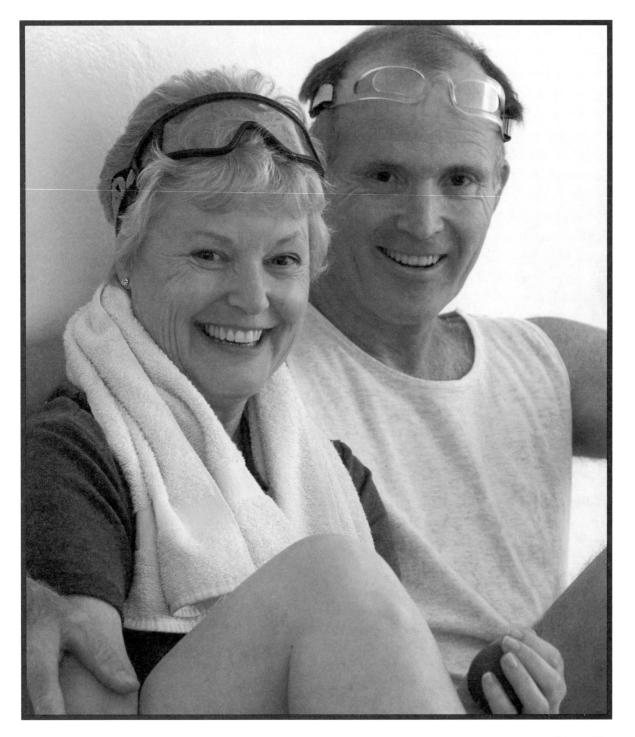

Do women get the same benefits from exercise as men?

healthy
living

How to
live well

SO...YOU'RE RETIRING AND NOW, FINALLY, it dawns on you that your health really is your greatest asset. Forget those fad diets and the latest hype about this vitamin or that supplement. Here are some basic, medically proven strategies for keeping you healthy:

EAT RIGHT As one ages, appetite and eating habits may change. Favorite foods may not taste the same. You may not be as hungry as you once were. Still, you need a healthy diet of varied foods to help ward off some of the adverse effects of aging on your body. Don't skimp when it comes to healthy, fresh food. (See page 180.)

EXERCISE No matter what your age, exercise can help you reduce your risk for stroke and heart attack, ward off mild depression, and give you a host of other healthy benefits. (See page 182.)

GET REGULAR CHECKUPS After the age of 45, everyone needs a comprehensive physical exam—annually—as an overall health check. Some important tests: mammogram (for women), prostate exam (for men), and colonoscopy (for both). Two major health indicators, blood pressure and cholesterol levels, will need regular monitoring (see below).

TREAT HIGH BLOOD PRESSURE Elevated blood pressure (or hypertension) is the leading risk factor for heart attacks, strokes, and kidney disease. It's more common in the elderly than the rest of the population. Unfortunately, high blood pressure often doesn't have early symptoms. That's why it's called the silent killer. A good strategy: Have your doctor check your blood pressure at every visit. You might also want to buy a home blood-pressure monitor and check it every week yourself.

KEEP YOUR CHOLESTEROL DOWN "Bad" cholesterol (or LDL) can cause a fatty buildup in your blood vessels. People with high LDL cholesterol are at greater risk of heart disease. Many people keep their cholesterol in check through regular exercise, a diet low in saturated fats, and by maintaining an appropriate body weight. There are also prescription medicines available to help lower your cholesterol.

STOP SMOKING By now, we all know that smoking can cause lung cancer. But smoking also increases your risk of other life-shortening health problems such as emphysema, heart disease, and stroke, as well as pancreatic and other types of cancer. Studies show that your risk for heart attack and stroke decreases when you kick the habit. Join a support group if you can't do it on your own, or talk to your doctor about taking medication to help you quit.

WATCH YOUR WEIGHT If you have a weight problem, you are not alone—one in three Americans is significantly overweight. Those extra pounds can make you feel sluggish, disrupt your sleep, cause heartburn—and put you at greater risk for high blood pressure, diabetes, heart disease, and some types of cancer. Extra weight also puts added stress on hips, knees, back, and ankles, and limits your mobility. Ask your doctor for advice if you can't get the extra weight off by yourself.

FIRST PERSON   SUCCESS STORY

Too Embarrassed to Avoid Cancer

I put off having a colonoscopy for years because I hated the idea of spending part of a day running to the bathroom during the preparation. The test requires you to take strong laxatives the day before the procedure. Finally, when I turned 55, my doctor said I really couldn't delay any longer. He also explained that I'd be given anesthesia, so I'd be drowsy and wouldn't feel a thing during the actual colonoscopy—something I didn't know. Well, I faced the music, and thank goodness I did, for several polyps were found during that procedure. They were removed painlessly before they could develop into tumors. The idea that I might have let them go any longer gives me shivers. I'm so glad I got over my silly embarrassment in time.

— Reese J., Reno, Nevada

eating
right

EATING A HEALTHY, BALANCED DIET can help you live a longer, healthier life. Research has proven, in fact, that eating right can control—and, in some cases, prevent—illnesses such as diabetes, heart disease, and high blood pressure. Now that you are retiring, you may have the time to shop more carefully and prepare more nutritious meals. But what foods should you eat exactly?

Vegetables are the core of a healthy diet. Two to three servings are imperative each day, but more is even better. Fruits, at least two a day, are also important. Juices are good, too, but they contain less fiber and their additional calories can add up.

It's simple— eat healthier foods

Six servings of whole grains, such as wheat, rice, oats, corn, and barley, are necessary components of every day's meal plan. Look for whole-grain breads and cereals for extra nutrition.

Dry beans (such as red or navy beans and soybeans) and other legumes (such as lentils and chickpeas) provide excellent sources of low-fat protein, especially when accompanied by a serving of bread or rice. Meat must be lean—and eaten infrequently—if you want to adhere to a healthy diet plan.

Dairy products keep bones in good shape. But as you age, an allergy to milk, called lactose intolerance, may develop. If it does, you need to eat other calcium-rich foods such as collard greens, spinach, and sardines. You'll also need more Vitamin D to help your body absorb the calcium in these foods. Fortified breakfast cereals and vitamin supplements designed for seniors can provide what you need.

FOOD PYRAMID FOR THE OLDER ADULT

Vitamin Supplements: Calcium, Vitamin D, Vitamin B-12

Fats, Oils, and Sweets: Use Sparingly

Meat, Poultry, Fish, Dried Beans, Eggs, and Nut Group: 3 servings

Milk, Yogurt, and Cheese Group: 3 servings

Fruit Group: 2 servings or more

Vegetable Group: 2-3 servings or more

Bread, Fortified Cereal, Rice, and Pasta Group: 6 servings

Fluids: 8 servings

Older people need fewer calories because they tend to be less active and their body composition changes. Nutrient needs stay the same—or even increase. To help older people select foods that provide the most nutrients, researchers at Tufts University recently drew a new food pyramid especially for 70-plus people. Note that its base is the commonly recommended eight glasses of water (or other fluids such as soup or juice) every day—a dietary component that's especially important for older people because their sense of thirst diminishes. That means they need to drink up, even when they don't feel thirsty.

exercise

Just a little bit will do

YES, RETIREMENT IS THE TIME TO SIT BACK and relax—but not all day. As you get older, you still need regular exercise. Exercise can:

- Prevent bone loss
- Lower your risk of many diseases associated with aging, such as heart disease, osteoporosis, and diabetes
- Improve balance and increase muscle strength
- Reduce stress, anxiety, and depression
- Help you feel better in general

This doesn't mean you must run a marathon or go in for advanced step aerobics. Just make moderate activity, such as walking or swimming, a daily part of your routine. Pick activities that are fun and that you can do year-round. To help you persevere, find a buddy to exercise with you. Some other guidelines to help you get moving:

- Check with your doctor before starting any exercise program.
- Wear comfortable, breathable clothing and appropriate shoes or sneakers.
- Take time to warm up and cool down. Stretch slowly. Your muscles lose elasticity as you age.
- Start slowly, and progress gradually. If you've been inactive lately, consider starting with less intense sports such as golf, croquet, shuffleboard, and table tennis.
- Brisk walking can be as beneficial as jogging, and it puts less stress on your knees, ankles, and heart. Choose a route that has a smooth surface, is well lit, and doesn't intersect with traffic. Many older Americans walk through shopping malls, which have the great advantage of being weatherproof.
- Try to do 30 minutes of continuous physical activity at least five days per week. Count activities such as gardening or raking leaves.
- Drink plenty of water, especially when exercising in hot, humid conditions. As you age, your sense of thirst decreases, so you can't simply wait until you feel thirsty to get a drink. Keep a large thermos of water nearby to remind you to drink up.

ASK THE EXPERTS

What's the right amount of exercise?

It depends on your activity level. If you've been inactive for a long while, then walking up and down the stairs is a good start. Ideally you want to build up to thirty minutes of moderate-level activity, such as an energetic walk, five times per week. The ideal exercise program should include endurance, strength, flexibility, and balance exercises (see box below).

Do women get the same benefits from exercise as men?

Most studies regarding exercise have been done with men, but the few studies that have included women indicate that women may benefit from exercise even more than men, because exercise, including weight training, helps fight osteoporosis. In addition, studies have shown that women who don't exercise have twice the chance of dying from heart disease as women who do exercise.

SENIOR EXERCISES

The National Institute on Aging has used available medical research to develop an Over-50 Fit Kit consisting of a 48-minute exercise video designed for older Americans to use at home. To receive a copy along with a 100-page instruction book, send a check or money order for $7, payable to the National Institute on Aging, to:

NIAIC, Dept. BR
P.O. Box 8057
Gaithersburg, MD 20898-8057

For more information, call 800-222-2225. You can read the book—and print it out from the Web site—at **www.maillist.org/exercise**.

recommended
checkups

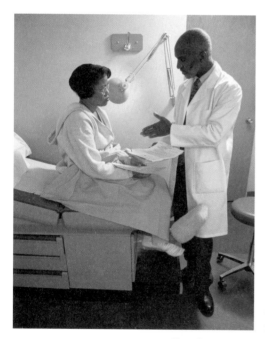

*Like a car, your body
needs regular tune-ups*

NO DOUBT, WHEN YOU TURNED 50
your doctor suggested you take various medical
screening tests. Now that you are retiring, make
these tests a top priority.

CANCER Tests can help doctors detect cancer early
and this gives them the best chance of treating the
disease successfully. These are three cancers that are
most common in older people:

Breast Cancer. In addition to monthly self-checks,
an important way to detect breast cancer is with a
mammogram—an x-ray that can detect tumors too
small to be felt in a physical exam. Women aged 50 and older should
have a mammogram every one to two years, unless your doctor recom-
mends them more often.

Colon Cancer. This is the second leading cause of death from cancer,
but it's one of the easiest to detect and cure with regular testing.
Starting at age 50 (40 if you have a family history) you should take two
tests—a fecal occult blood test and either a sigmoidoscopy or
colonoscopy—to detect colon cancer.

Prostate Cancer. This is a threat to men over age 50, African-
American men, and men with a family history of prostate cancer. An
annual exam and a PSA (that's Prostate Specific Antigen) blood test can
help detect prostate cancer.

HIGH CHOLESTEROL Cholesterol is an artery-clogging fat that swims in your blood and can cause heart disease. Cholesterol levels can be monitored with blood tests. Note: It can rise significantly in middle-aged men, women on the cusp of menopause, and people who gain weight.

DIABETES The chances of developing diabetes increases after age 45. Your doctor will want to give you a blood test for it if you are overweight, had gestational diabetes during a pregnancy, or have a family member with diabetes.

OSTEOPOROSIS As you age, you may develop osteoporosis, a condition in which the bones tend to become brittle and break more easily. A bone-density test, which is done using a type of X ray machine, can indicate if you have this problem. This condition is much more common in older women than men. It is usually treated with a calcium-rich diet, strength exercises, calcium supplements, and medications.

HEARING LOSS Hearing loss increases after age 50. You may find that you have to strain to hear a normal conversation or that you must turn up the volume of the TV. Testing is important at the onset of the smallest hearing problems, because hearing aids are easier to get used to if you start to wear them earlier rather than later.

VISION PROBLEMS Once you turn 45 or so, your vision may undergo some changes. For example, you may find it's getting harder to read fine print. You need an annual vision test and eye exam to stay on top of these age-related changes. You may need to start wearing reading glasses or some other type of corrective lenses. **Glaucoma**, a disease with no symptoms that you can detect without a medical exam, can lead to serious vision problems, even blindness. But if it's discovered early on, it can be treated with medicine, surgery, or both. **Cataracts** can cloud your vision after the age of 60, but can usually be handled with outpatient procedures.

IMMUNIZATIONS

Shots aren't just for kids. Older adults need them to prevent disease, too. Ask your doctor about the following immunizations:

Influenza (flu) Once you turn 65, your doctor may suggest this shot every year.

Pneumonia You get this shot just once—usually at about age 65.

Tetanus-Diphtheria Booster Everyone needs this shot every 10 years.

Hepatitis B Talk to your doctor about this one-time-only vaccine. You generally need it only if you have had blood transfusions or were a healthcare worker who was exposed to blood or blood products.

memory loss

*Forgetfulness
is okay*

FORGETFULNESS IS A NORMAL BYPRODUCT whenever you suffer from stress, anxiety, loneliness, or boredom. Retirement can incorporate all of those aspects, as can moving from your home or coping with the death of a spouse or friend. Fortunately, forgetfulness caused by these reactions is usually temporary, and goes away when the stress fades.

Chronic, life-inhibiting forgetfulness is a different story. Alzheimer's disease and dementia don't go away. As its name implies, **Alzheimer's disease** is a progressive brain disease in which healthy brain tissue degenerates, causing a steady decline in memory and mental abilities. And it's more than simple forgetfulness. Alzheimer's disease may start with slight memory loss and confusion—but it leads to severe, irreversible mental impairment that destroys a person's ability to remember most things, including the names and faces of family members. Over time, the sufferer becomes so incapacitated that he can no longer perform daily activities. Some good news: There are now medications that slow the course of the disease in certain cases.

Dementia (or senility, as it used to be called) can be due to a number of medical problems. Strokes and other circulatory disorders can impair memory. That's why older people who are worried by forgetfulness should be tested by a doctor who specializes in age-related memory problems. If such a specialist is not available in your area, then look for a **gerontologist**, a doctor who studies aging. Thanks to new medications, some cases of dementia can be arrested and even reversed.

KEEP YOUR MEMORY SHARP

If you suffer from memory lapses following major surgery or a bout of loneliness, anxiety, or boredom, you can bring your memory back up to speed by sharpening your mental skills. According to the National Institute on Aging, the following measures can help you exercise your mind and get it in better working condition:

- Stay involved in activities that stimulate both the mind and the body.
- Exercise. It can help you retain a healthy state of mind.
- Limit the use of alcoholic beverages. Over time, heavy drinking can cause permanent brain damage.
- Plan tasks ahead of time. Make things-to-do lists, for example, and use notes, calendars, and other memory aids.
- Remember things by mentally connecting them to other meaningful items, such as a familiar name, song, or lines from a poem.

EXPERIENCE COUNTS

People who suffer from Alzheimer's disease lose their abilities at different rates, but some common signs of the disease include:
- Increasing and persistent forgetfulness
- An inability to follow directions
- Disorientation; becoming lost in familiar places
- Neglecting personal safety, hygiene, and nutrition
- Mood swings (sufferers often withdraw socially)
- An inability to perform everyday tasks such as brushing teeth or cooking

If these symptoms show up, see a neurologist, preferably one who specializes in geriatric memory problems. Other illnesses—some of them quite treatable—can cause memory problems, including vitamin deficiencies, stroke, and depression.

grief

Any loss must be mourned

LOSING A LOVED ONE CAN FEEL as if a part of yourself has been torn out. It can be even more overwhelming if you've just retired and lose a spouse soon after. Not only has your mate died, but your dreams of retired life together are lost, too. Many people describe it as being on an emotional roller-coaster, where intense feelings of shock, anger, disbelief, denial, extreme sadness, and emptiness fluctuate during the various stages of mourning.

Most of the more intense symptoms associated with acute grief will generally begin to subside after three to twelve months. In the period immediately following a loss, for example, you may feel numb. Often, it takes a great effort to eat, sleep, or even breathe. It may help to think about grief as being similar to an illness, and allow it to run its course without becoming too anxious about how long it is taking to heal.

Does grief ever actually end? In general, it is believed that it takes anywhere from two to six years after a loss of a close family member—a spouse, sibling, parent, or child—for most people to feel like themselves again. Moments of sadness can recur—especially on significant holidays, anniversary dates, or when you hear that special song you both enjoyed on the radio. But as time passes, the sadness and longing will be less intense.

You'll know you're getting better, in fact, when you find that you're looking forward to the future and making plans; when you're meeting new people and developing new interests; when you actually believe that your life as a retiree will go on—and when certain memories make you smile instead of breaking into tears.

GETTING THROUGH IT

Grieving the loss of a spouse or loved one is a painful, life-changing event. At some point or other, most mourners wonder, "How am I going to get through this?" Like most problems, the answer depends on your personality. Here are some ways to cope:

- Read self-help books. There are a host of good books available on how to deal with loss.
- Keep a journal. Writing lets you express your grief in a very personal and private way.
- Talk to a close friend or relative or your spiritual counselor (a pastor or rabbi). Sharing your feelings with them can help you get through this trying time.
- Join a bereavement group if you don't feel like talking to friends or relatives, or if you prefer to talk to other people who are experiencing the same problem. Sponsored by hospitals, churches, and other community organizations, these support groups let mourners talk regularly with others who are in similar situations. (For a group in your area, contact AARP: 800-424-3410 or **griefandloss@aarp.org**.)
- See a grief counselor. If you feel uncomfortable opening up in a group, an individual counselor can give you support. If possible, find someone who specializes in bereavement.

LOSING THINGS OTHER THAN PEOPLE

A milder version of grief can occur when losses other than a loved one's death occur. Divorce can be an occasion for grief. Moving from a beloved home can cause grieving, as can the change of a way of life. Retirement can bring on a kind of grief if the job was very enjoyable. Some people who are uprooted from city life grieve for it, even when they find themselves in a bucolic paradise. And similarly, people who love country life might long for that if they find themselves in the city. The loss of one's health to a severe, chronic illness may bring on a period of mourning.

depression

*Depression
is not a
normal part
of aging*

MOST DEPRESSION IS AN EMOTIONAL reaction to an
unhappy event. It's natural to feel depressed after the death of a loved one,
for example, or during a divorce proceeding or following the loss of a job,
which can be how some people view retirement. But when the sadness goes
on too long or gets too painful, it's cause for concern.

Serious depression, also known as **clinical depression**, is an illness that
affects your ability to function in everyday life—and often must be treated
with medication or therapy. Because older people may experience more
losses in later life, such as a decline in their health or the death of friends
and family, they are at risk for developing depression. Often, the symptoms of depression are overlooked (and go untreated) because their onset
coincides with other chronic illnesses common in later life such as diabetes, stroke, heart disease, cancer, chronic lung disease, Alzheimer's disease, and arthritis. Fortunately, clinical depression can be treated successfully in over 80% of all cases.

WARNING SIGNS OF DEPRESSION

Sadness is only one sign of clinical depression. If you suffer from five or
more of the following symptoms for more than two weeks, you should
consult your doctor:

- Loss of interest in normal daily activities
- Feelings of helplessness or worthlessness
- Difficulty sleeping, or sleeping too much
- An increased appetite and weight gain, or a reduced appetite and
  weight loss
- Loss of energy; extreme fatigue
- Difficulty making decisions, concentrating, or remembering
- Restlessness; a constant state of agitation
- Constant thoughts of suicide and death

ASK THE EXPERTS

Which illnesses can contribute to depression?

Studies reveal a link between depression and heart disease. Depression occurs in up to half of those who have had heart attacks. An underactive thyroid (hypothyroidism)—even a very mild condition—can also cause depression.

My family has never had any mental problems. Is there any way I can feel better without having to tell a doctor about my problems?

Depression is not a character flaw that you should feel guilty or ashamed about. It can't be remedied by merely "getting over it." It is a real, medical illness. Fortunately, it is treatable. If you experience symptoms of depression (see opposite page), contact your physician. As a first step, he may recommend a thorough physical exam to rule out other illnesses. Treatment for depression may include antidepressant medication and/or psychiatric counseling. Psychotherapy often helps people cope with ongoing problems that trigger or contribute to the depression.

I've heard that people use alcohol, nicotine, or drugs to medicate an underlying depression. Is that true?

Experts once thought that people with depression used alcohol, nicotine, and mood-altering drugs as a way to ease depression. But studies now show that using these substances may actually contribute to depression.

Where can I get more information about depression?

Contact these sources for more information: The Campaign on Clinical Depression: 800-228-1114, and the Depression Awareness, Recognition and Treatment Program (DART) at the National Institutes of Health: 800-421-4211.

now what do I do?
Answers to common questions

Is there a medical facility where I can go for a complete checkup of everything?

The famed Mayo Clinic in Rochester, Minnesota, offers one-stop shopping. For two days you'll undergo marathon tests that add up to an exhaustive physical exam. The test results will be discussed with you before you leave the clinic. Several other large medical centers offer similar arrangements; ask your doctor to recommend the one nearest you. Not all insurers cover these tests; check with your healthcare provider if you aren't prepared to pay for it out of pocket.

I have an older relative who has trouble seeing, but I can't get her to go to an eye doctor. I think she worries about the money. Where can she go for help?

The National Eye Care Project, funded by the Foundation of the American Academy of Ophthalmology and the Knights Templar Eye Foundation, offers free eye care to U.S. citizens aged 65 and older who have not seen an ophthalmologist in the last three years (800-222-3937). You get a comprehensive eye exam from a volunteer ophthamologist and treatment for any condition diagnosed for up to one year. The doctor will accept Medicare and/or other insurance reimbursement as payment in full. Patients without insurance receive care at no charge. (Patients who are in an HMO or who obtain care through the VA or the armed services are not eligible.)

My husband died nine months ago. I'm just starting to feel less numb, but the holidays are coming up. How am I ever going to get through them without him?

The holidays can be an especially painful time when you're grieving. Take some time now to plan ahead. It'll help ease the strain on the holiday itself. Establish some new traditions. This can take the focus off the the way you and your husband used to do things. But don't be afraid to talk to others about your sad feelings (yes, even at this happy time) or about your husband. If possible, volunteer. At a time like this, it often feels good to give a helping hand to others. Most of all, be patient with yourself. You may not be able to celebrate as merrily this year (or even next year) as you have done in the past. But over time, you'll find the pain will ease.

My wife has been diagnosed with Alzheimer's, and I feel overwhelmed. Is there anyone who can help me manage this situation?

Older people often end up as caregivers for loved ones with chronic disorders, and it can be physically and emotionally challenging. But there are more resources to help you than ever before. National associations for specific illnesses offer information to keep you abreast of the newest research and alternative treatments. (Ask your librarian to help you find the name and address of the one you need, or search for it on the Internet.) Different support groups for caregivers and patients meet regularly—in person and on the Internet. They can help with the day-to-day problems that arise with a chronic illness.

Now where do I go?!

CONTACTS

AARP (**www.aarp.org**) has a list of 100 Web sites on health and medicine (dealing with everything from depression and mental illness to diabetes and Alzheimer's disease) with links that enable you to go directly to any site that interests you.

The Mayo Clinic's site (**www.mayohealth.com**) is a virtual encyclopedia, chock-full of reader-friendly information on every disease, medical condition, drug, and therapy from A to Z.

For dealing with grief, these sites offer advice, chat rooms, and helpful articles:
- **www.counselingforloss.com**
- **www.fortnet.org/WidowNet**
- **www.rivendell.org**; and **www.death-dying.com**

BOOKS

On Death and Dying
Death: The Final Stage of Growth
by Dr. Elisabeth Kubler-Ross
Both of these books are considered classics on dealing with death.

Get a Life: You Don't Need a Million to Retire
by Ralph Warner
An inspiring discussion of the key steps—such as developing authentic interests and friendships—you can take to ensure a fulfilling retirement.

Aging Well
by Harvard professors Jeanne Wei and Sue Levkoff
This book discusses medical science in layman's terms.

glossary

Activities of Daily Living (ADLs)—These activities trigger long-term care insurance benefits. Examples include eating, transferring (in and out of bed, chairs), dressing, bathing, and using the toilet.

Adjusted Gross Income (AGI)—This is a tax term for all of your income (salary, interest, dividends, retirement income, etc.), adjusted for certain items, like contributions to IRAs and self-employed retirement plans, alimony payments, deductible student loan interest, and deductible moving expenses. The significance? It's used in many calculations to figure out if you can take certain deductions and credits.

Annuity—This is an investment that guarantees income payments to its owner for the owner's lifetime. When an investor buys an annuity (using after-tax dollars), his investment grows tax deferred until he begins to withdraw money from the account. Of course, there's a cost to the guaranteed income and the tax-deferred growth. Commissions, administrative fees, surrender charges, and early withdrawal penalties often make annuities a wise investment for only a small number of people.

Assisted Living—This hybrid housing alternative is similar to independent-living arrangements and also contains elements of a nursing home, such as help with activities of daily living (ADLs).

Beneficiary—Just a few letters shy of the word "benefits," the beneficiary is the person who benefits from being named on an investor's retirement account (IRA, 401(k), SEP IRA) or life insurance policy: if the owner dies, the money transfers to the beneficiary named.

Bond—Essentially a loan from a government or company to an individual, a bond is a promise to pay a fixed amount of interest for the use of someone else's money for a fixed period of time. For this reason, bonds are known as fixed income investments.

Capital Gains Tax—When stocks increase in value, the profit you make is called a capital gain. If you sell the stock, you owe tax—the capital gains tax—on the difference between the price you paid for it and the price you sold it for. This tax generally applies to any investment you sell for more than you paid. If you hold your investment for more than one year, the capital gain is considered long-term and is taxed at better rates than your other income. If you hold it less than one year, it's considered short-term, and is taxed just like your other income.

Chronic Illness—An illness that lasts more than three months is considered to be chronic. More than 90 million Americans live with chronic illnesses such as arthritis, cancer, diabetes, and heart disease.

Clinical Depression—A feeling of pervasive sadness that must be treated with medication and/or therapy. Other symptoms include a loss of interest in daily activities and a marked change in appetite or sleeping patterns. Depression can be triggered by other chronic illnesses common in later life such as diabetes, stroke, and arthritis.

Continuing Care Retirement Communities (CCRCs)—These communities combine independent living, assisted living, and nursing home care all in one location, allowing seniors to "age in place" without moving every time their situation changes.

Credit Shelter Trust—Also known as a Bypass Trust or an A-B Trust, this estate-tax-saving trust allows the first $675,000 of a person's estate to flow into a trust for the kids (or other heirs), rather than going right to the surviving spouse. Any assets over the $675,000 flow to the surviving spouse. When the spouse dies, the $675,000 exclusion will be used again, so a total of $1,350,000 will escape tax.

Defined Benefit Pension Plan—This is a fancy name for a retirement plan that pays longtime employees a specific amount of money (a defined benefit) each month once they retire. It's highly desirable, since employees don't have to contribute any money to this plan in order to benefit from it.

Defined Contribution Pension Plan—This is a fancy name for a 401(k) or similar plan. These plans generally rely on you (the employee) to make regular (defined) contributions to your own account, which grows tax-deferred until you need the money, usually after retirement. The amount you receive at retirement depends on how much you invested in the plan over the years and how well the account's investments performed.

Dividend—An added bonus to some stock investments, dividends are a part of a company's profits returned to the shareholders. Mutual funds also pay dividends to their shareholders, based on the income of the fund's underlying stocks and bonds.

Early Retirement—The traditional retirement age is 65. If you retire before this time, it's considered early retirement. The amount you receive in a pension and/or Social Security benefits may be affected if you take early retirement. You may also be penalized if you withdraw money from an IRA or a 401(k) plan before age $59^1/_2$.

Estate Planning—Not something only for the superrich, estate planning is the process of planning for the disposition and administration of assets at a person's death (or mental or physical incapacity), which is something that applies to many people.

Estate Tax—If you die with "too much" money and you don't qualify for certain deductions, the IRS will levy estate taxes on the assets you leave behind. You're allowed to leave as much as you want to your spouse or to charity, and the first $675,000 beyond that is also exempt. But after that, this hefty tax—37% to 55%—kicks in.

Executor—This is the person named in a will to handle all of a deceased person's financial affairs, or estate.

Fixed Income—See Bond

Group Travel—These educational, cultural, historical, and athletic adventures let you see the world with other similar-age folks who share your interests.

Independent Living—These retirement communities are geared toward mobile older folks who want to remain independent but who want to live in a community with their peer group, and may want the convenience of prepared meals, housekeeping, and activities.

Individual Retirement Account—See IRA

Inflation—This measures how fast the prices of goods and services are rising.

Institutes for Learning in Retirement—These courses, offered on many college campuses to students age 50 and older, are inexpensive and don't have tests or grades. Topics range from Chaucer and computers to history and yoga.

IRA—Investors use Individual Retirement Accounts to stash money for retirement. Interest and dividends that are earned in this type of account aren't taxed until you withdraw the money, usually after retirement.

Itemized Deductions—Mortgage interest, real estate taxes, charitable contributions, and state income taxes add up to significant tax reductions. Even though it can mean a more complicated tax return, it's often more beneficial than taking the standard deduction.

Life Insurance—In exchange for annual payments (or "premiums"), a life insurance company will issue a contract (or "policy") that promises to pay a fixed amount when the policy's owner dies. The payment is made to the person listed in the policy as the beneficiary. Term policy premiums stay low for a fixed number of years (usually 5 to 30), then usually rise dramatically if the owner wants to keep the policy in place. Permanent policy premiums start out higher than term premiums, but stay level for the owner's entire lifetime. Permanent policies also have a savings component, called the cash value, which builds over time.

Living Trust—Living trusts are like wills, but they allow any assets held by the trust to avoid probate and pass directly to your heirs. However, they are often more costly to create than wills and more burdensome to manage during your lifetime.

Long-Term Care Insurance—This type of health insurance picks up costs that traditional health insurance does not, such as an extended stay in a nursing home or nursing care in your own home. This type of insurance is expensive, especially if you buy it when you're 60 years of age or older.

Long-Term Capital Gain—See Capital Gains Tax

Lump Sum Distribution—At retirement, you can often withdraw the entire balance of your retirement plan in one single payment. Frequently, retirees then put this "lump" into a rollover IRA.

Medicaid—This health insurance provides free coverage for low-income people of any age. You may also qualify for Medicaid if you are disabled.

Medicare—This health insurance for people age 65 and older is offered by the federal government at low or no cost. Medicare doesn't cover all medical costs, and it pays only a portion of the costs of many services. Medicare has two parts: Part A and Part B. (See Medicare Part A and Medicare Part B.)

Medicare Part A—This hospital insurance covers hospital stays, hospice care, and some home healthcare.

Medicare Part B—This medical insurance covers most doctors' services, medical equipment, and supplies.

Medigap—This supplemental insurance policy fills the "gap" between the medical coverage that Medicare offers and the coverage that many people need. There are ten standard medigap policies. Each policy, ranging from letter A to letter J, offers additional benefits.

Nursing Homes—These long-term care (or skilled nursing) facilities provide 24-hour support for people with chronic and long-term illnesses who can't live independently. They generally provide a full range of services, including daily nursing care, and dietary and therapeutic assistance.

Pension Plans—See Defined Benefit Plan and Defined Contribution Plan

Power of Attorney—A written, legally binding document that gives another person the right to make financial or health decisions on your behalf.

Probate—This is the long and winding road heirs must follow through the court system to carry out the deceased's wishes, as made known in his or her will.

Required Minimum Distributions—These are the withdrawals the IRS requires you to start taking out of your IRAs, annuities, and other retirement accounts once you reach age $70^1/_2$. Failure to comply will cost you a 50% penalty!

Reverse Mortgage—This is the payment(s) the bank makes to you, based on the equity in your home. It doesn't need to be repaid until your house is sold, typically after your death, when your heirs sell the home. Common types of reverse mortgages include Tenure Reverse Mortgages, where you receive monthly payments for the rest of your life, regardless of how long you live; Term Reverse Mortgages, where you receive a fixed number of monthly payments; and a Line of Credit Reverse Mortgage, where you receive a specified line of credit that you may draw on.

Risk—Your investment might not increase as you expect it to; or worse, it could end up losing money. This possibility is known as risk. Investors accept risk, however, because they believe that the possible payoff (or "return") ultimately will be worthwhile.

Rollover—At retirement, you can take the money from your 401(k) in one lump-sum distribution. Trouble is, you'll owe taxes on that money—all at once. A smarter strategy is to *roll over* the money directly from your former employer's 401(k) plan into an IRA. That way, you'll still have complete control of the funds yet the money will continue to grow tax-deferred until withdrawal.

Roth IRA—Named after the senator who invented it, the Roth IRA is an individual retirement account that doesn't allow an up-front deduction (like a traditional IRA). Instead, this nifty IRA uses after-tax dollars to fund it, so when the money is withdrawn during retirement, the investor doesn't have to pay tax on the money it earned over the years.

Short-Term Capital Gain—See Capital Gains Tax

Spousal Benefits—Social Security benefits that your spouse (or ex-spouse) can collect, based on your earnings. These are usually one-half of your benefit.

Standard Deduction—If you don't list out (or "itemize") your deductions on your income tax return, you can take the standard deduction, which is a minimum fixed deduction amount that all taxpayers are entitled to deduct.

Stock—This is a type of investment that represents ownership in a company.

Survivor Rights—When you die, your spouse will get at least half the pension benefit that you were receiving. If you pick the single-life option, however, you waive your survivor rights.

Tax Credit—Certain credits are allowed to offset your tax bill, dollar for dollar. Examples of these credits include a $600 credit for each child under age 17; income tax paid to a foreign government; and education credits for certain college costs for you or your children.

Trust—This is a very general term that describes a wide range of vehicles used to own property. Trusts generally don't save money on taxes. They're used mostly when someone wants to put restrictions or parameters on how their property is used, managed, and distributed to others.

Will—This basic legal document specifies who gets your money and property after you die. It also names the person who will handle your affairs (the executor, or the estate administrator), and names a guardian for any minor children.

index

A

AARP (American Association of Retired
      Persons), 17, 34, 65, 193
    Home Equity Information Center, 59
    pamphlets, 73
    and travel discounts, 82
    and volunteer work, 81
about.com, 65
A-B trusts, 171
Access-Able Travel Source, 89
Accessible Journeys, 89
Accessible Tours, 89
Accessible Vacation Home Exchange, 89
Administration on Aging, 123
airlines, senior discounts, 82
Alzheimer's disease, 186, 187
    spouse diagnosed with, 193
American Academy of Estate Planning, 175
American Association of Homes and Services
      for the Aging, 73
American Association of Individual
      Investors, 39
American Association of Retired Persons.
      See AARP
American Citizens Abroad, 62
America's 100 Best Places to Retire (Fox), 65
annuities, 134–135
    publications, 137
annuitized payments
    401(k)s, 111
    pension, 118–119
Arkansas, 70
assets, 24
    allocation, 29
assisted living, 66
    coverage by insurance, 72
attorney, choosing, 174

B

bad-debt syndrome, 44
Barnes & Noble, 87

beneficiary, 168, 169
bereavement groups, 189
Better Business Bureaus, 49
bonds, 127, 135, 136
books. *See* publications
403(b) plans, 107, 123
breast cancer, 184
budgets, 38, 46
burial vaults, 173
business, starting your own, 79
bypass trusts, 171

C

Campaign on Clinical Depression, 191
cancer, 184
capital gains, 127
    stocks and, 174
capital losses, 127
caregivers, 193
cars, 35
    insurance, 157
cataracts, 185
certificates of deposit (CDs), 126
certified public accountant, 37
charitable donations, 171
chartered life underwriter, 37
checking accounts, 126
children of first marriage, providing for, 174
cholesterol, 179, 185
cliff vesting, 117
clinical depression, 190–191
codicils, 165
college courses, 86
college towns as retirement place, 65
colon cancer, 184
colonoscopy, 178, 179
community groups, 77
Consolidated Omnibus Budget Reconciliation
      Act (COBRA), 148, 149
consolidation loans, 51
consulting, 13, 79

Consumer Credit Counseling Services, 47
consumer watchdogs, 49
Continental Casualty, 153
Continuing Care Accreditation
        Commission, 67
continuing care retirement communities, 66–67
cost, 67
cost cutting, 34–35
coworkers, missing, 11
Cox, Dennis, 85
credit cards
    debt, 42–43, 50, 51
    as emergency cash, 45
    finding cheaper, 35, 43, 45
    interest, 42
    limiting to one, 45
    not using, 44–45
    transferring balances, 35, 43, 45
credit counselors, 46
    finding, 47
credit for elderly, 33
creditors, harassment by, 50
credit ratings, 47
credits (Social Security), 92
credit shelter trusts, 171

D

death
    dying intestate, 162
    IRAs and, 131
    publications, 193
debt
    getting out of, 40–51
    and house equity, 57
    publications, 51
    what to pay first, 50
Debtors Anonymous, 44
deductible IRA, 128
defined benefits, 117
dementia, 186
depression, 15, 190–191

Depression Awareness, Recognition and
        Treatment Program (DART), 191
diabetes, 185
disability insurance, 101, 157
Disabled Directory, 89
divorce, 189
    ex-husband's pension, 119

E

early retirement, 12–13
    assessing package, 17
    and health insurance, 148
    and 401(k)s, 113
    and pension plans, 121
early withdrawals
    IRAs, 12, 129, 137
    401(k)s, 12
    Roth IRAs, 32
    SIMPLEs, 115
Earthwatch Institute, 83
eating right, 178, 180–181
education, 86–87
    lifetime learning, 65
    traveling and, 84
Elderhostel, 84
Elderhostel Service Programs, 83
Eldertreks, 85
Employee Retirement Income Security Act
        (ERISA), 122
estate planning, 158–175
    identifying assets and liabilities, 161
    regular reviews of, 165
estate taxes, 170
    minimizing, 163, 171
    repeal of, 174
European Walking Tours, 85
excess accumulation, 130
executor, 164–165, 169
    choosing, 165
    payment of, 165
exercise, 178, 182–183

men compared to women, 183
   right amount of, 183
extended term life insurance, 141
eyecare, 185
   free, 192

F

Facts for Consumers: Reverse Mortgages
      (F TC), 59
family history, writing, 77
Fannie Mae, 59
Federal Trade Commission (FTC), 39, 50, 59
   and scams, 49
Fidelity National Financial, Inc., 153
finances, 20–39. *See also* estate planning
   continual review of, 27
   and existing home, 56
   getting in order, 20–21
   and place of retirement, 54
   publications, 39
   standard advice, 28
financial analyst, certified, 37
financial planners, 36–37
   certified, 37
   fees, 36
   locating, 37
Financial Planning Association, 37
Flying Wheels, 89
food pyramid, 181
forgetfulness, 186
Foundation of the American Academy of
      Ophthalmology, 192
Fox, Richard L., 65
freelancing, 79
FTC. *See* Federal Trade Commission
full retirement age, 94
funeral expenses, 173
   lifetime term insurance to pay for, 141
   prepaying, 172
funeral parlors, 174
funeral planning, 172–173

publications, 175

G

Garrett Planning Network, 37
gifts, 171
glaucoma, 185
Global Access Disabled Travel Network, 89
Global Volunteers, 83
glossary of terms, 194–197
graded vesting, 117
Grand Travel, 84–85
grantor, 168, 169
grave liners, 173
grief, 188–189
   counselor, 189
   holidays and, 192
   Web sites dealing with, 193
group life policy, 141
guaranteed payment annuity, 119

H

Habitat for Humanity International, 81
health
   and existing home, 56
   healthy living, 178–185
   and place of retirement, 54
healthcare insurance, 146–149
   fee-for-service plan, 146
   former employer's plan, 148
   health maintenance organization (HMO), 147
   individual policy, 148, 149
   paying for, 148–149
   point-of-service plan, 146
   preferred-provider, 146, 147
   publications, 157
   traditional indemnity, 146
healthcare power of attorney, 167
Health Insurance Portability and
      Accountability Act (HIPAA), 148
Health Maintenance Organizations
      (HMOs), 147

health services not covered by Medicare, 143

Health Volunteers Overseas, 83

hearing loss, 185

heart disease, depression and, 191

hepatitis B vaccine, 185

high blood pressure, 178

high schools, adult education courses at, 86

HIPAA (Health Insurance Portability and
        Accountability Act), 148

HMOs, 147

hobbies, 76

   cost of new, 76

   turning into a business, 13

home

   keeping existing one, 56–57

   publications, 73

   renting, 63

   selling, 33, 60–61, 72

   sharing, 63

   swapping, 57

HomeExchange, 57

*Home Keeper: It Pays to Keep You in Your
        Home* (FannieMae), 59

HomeLink U.S.A., 57

hospitalization

   part A of Medicare, 142

   standard Medigap plans, 145

household items, selling, 38

HUD, 59

I

immediate annuity, 134, 135

immunizations, 185

income, 24

   below living expenses, 26, 27

   sample income sheet, 25

independent living, 66

individual retirement accounts. See IRAs

inflation, 26, 27, 28

   and long-term care policies, 153

   pensions and, 121

influenza shots, 185

inheritance, 33

Institutes for Learning in Retirement, 87

insurance. *See also* disability insurance;
        healthcare insurance; life insurance;
        long-term care insurance; Medigap
        insurance

   beneficiary designations, 160

   needs, 138–157

   publications, 137, 157

   reviewing coverage, 35

Internal Revenue Service. *See* IRS

International Cemetery and Funeral
        Association, 175

International Executive Service Corps, 83

investments

   diversification, 29

   publications, 137

   and retirement, 28

involuntary conservatorship, 167

IRAs, 128–133

   beginning withdrawal process, 131

   beneficiary designations, 131, 160

   converting regular to Roth, 133

   death and, 131

   early withdrawals, 12, 129, 137

   required minimum distributions (RMDs),
        130, 131

   rolling 401(k)s into, 108, 109

IRS (Internal Revenue Service)

   form 8606, 129

   publication 590, 130

   publications, 33

J

job. *See also* second careers

   missing, 10

   part-time, 79

   salary and Social Security payments, 99

John Hancock, 153

joint and survivor annuity, 118–119

K

Keogh retirement plan, 114
    required minimum distributions (RMDs),
       115
Knights Templar Eye Foundation, 192
401(k)s, 106–113
    annuitized distributions, 111
    borrowing money from, 122
    early withdrawals, 12
    employer's contribution, 106
    lump-sum distribution, 108–109
    monthly income from, 111
    remaining with employer, 110–111
    required minimum distribution (RMD),
       112–113

L

life insurance, 140–141
    benefits, 33
    cash value, 140
    publications, 157
    tapping into, 156
lifestyle
    and existing home, 56
    and place of retirement, 54
lifetime term insurance, 141
line of credit reverse mortgage, 58
living abroad, 62
living trusts, 168
    as compared to wills, 169
living wills, 163
    as opposed to healthcare power of attorney,
       167
longevity, 176–193
long-term capital gain, 127
long-term care insurance, 72, 150–153
    assessing, 153
    benefits, 153
    buying, 152–153
    life insurance companies offering, 153

    limitations and exclusions, 156
    pre-existing health problems, 156
lump-sum payments
    401(k)s, 108–109
    pensions, 120–121, 122
    variable annuity, 134, 135

M

Malaca Instituto, 85
mammogram, 178
Managed Care Medicare plan, 147
Marine Toys for Tots Foundation, 81
Mass Mutual, 153
Mayo Clinic, 192
    Web site, 193
Medicaid, 154–155
    and assisted living, 72
    as distinguished from Medicare, 142, 154
    long-term care services covered by, 155
    and nursing home care, 151
    spending down and, 155
medical checkups, 178, 184–185
    complete checkups, 192
medical expenses, 33
    Part B of Medicare, 142
    standard Medigap plans, 145
Medicare, 102, 142–143
    applying for, 96
    and assisted living, 72
    claims, 157
    as distinguished from Medicaid, 154
    enrolling in, 1443
    and living abroad, 62
    and nursing home care, 151
    optional part, 142, 143
    and preferred-provider health plans, 147
    publications, 157
Medicare + Choice, 143
Medicare Select plan, 147
Medigap insurance, 144–145
    advantages of buying early, 156

compared to Medicare managed care plan, 147

standard plans, 145

memory loss, 186–187

Modern Maturity, 65

money. *See* finances

Money, 65, 73

money market accounts, 126

money market mutual funds, 126, 136

monthly payments

401(k)s, 111

pensions, 122

mortgages. See also reverse mortgages

paying off, 32, 57

refinancing, 72

moving, 57, 62–65

to foreign countries, 62

and grief, 189

taxes, 70–71

mutual funds, 127

N

National Association of Financial & Estate Planning, 175

National Association of Personal Financial Advisors, 37

National Center for Home Equity Conversion, 59

National Council on Aging, 153

National Eye Care Project, 192

National Foundation for Consumer Credit, 47

National Institute on Aging, 183, 187

National Network of Estate Planning Attorneys, 175

National Resource Center on Supportive Housing and Home Modification, 73

National Reverse Mortgage Lenders Association, 59

National Shared Housing Resource Center, 61

nondeductible IRA, 129

North Carolina Center for Creative Retirement (NCCCR), 65

nursing homes, 66

Medicaid and, 151, 155

Medicare and, 151

O

Odysseys Unlimited, 85

online courses, 87

osteoporosis, 185

Over-50 Fit Kit, 183

Over the Hill Gang, International, 85

P

paperwork

applying for Social Security, 97

and Medicare claims, 157

and move to congregate-living facility, 67

partner, 14–15, 16

paycheck, missing, 11

Pension Benefit Guaranty Corporation (PBGC), 121, 122

pensions, 21, 116–121

annuity payments, 118–119

fixed benefit formula, 121

inflation and, 121

lump-sum payments, 120–121, 122

monthly payments, 122

taxes, 117

unit benefit formula, 121

permanent insurance. *See* whole-life insurance

Personal Earnings & Benefit Estimate Statement (PES), 93

personal loans, 51

Photo Explorer Tours, 85

place of retirement, 52–73

best places, 64

publications, 73

rating of, 55

pneumonia shots, 185

Points of Light Foundation, 81

power of attorney, 166–167

principal

leaving untouched, 24

spending, 30
probate court, 162
    avoiding, 165
property power of attorney, 166
prostate
    cancer, 184
    exam, 178
public assistance, 33
publications, 89
    aging well, 193
    annuities, 137, 157
    death and dying, 193
    debt, 51
    finances, 39, 175
    funerals, 175
    health insurance, 157
    home planning, 73
    insurance, 137, 157
    investment, 137
    IRS, 33
    401(k)s, 123
    life insurance, 157
    Medicare, 157
    places to retire, 73
    preparing for retirement, 17, 193
    retirement plans, 123
    Social security benefits, 103

Q

qualified terminable interest property trust
    (Q-TIP), 174
"Questions You Should Ask About Your
    Investments" (SEC), 49

R

reading, 88
required minimum distributions (RMDs)
    calculating, 131
    exceptions, 113, 115
    IRAs, 130, 131
    401(k)s, 112–113

    Keogh retirement plan, 115
    SEPs, 114, 115
    SIMPLEs, 114
RE-SEED, 87
resort communities, 62
Retirees Enhancing Science Education
    Through Experiments and
    Demonstration, 87
retirement communities, 66
    choosing, 72
    evaluating, 68–69
retirement myths, 9
Retirement Places Rated (Savageau), 65
retirement planning
    publications, 17, 123, 193
    worksheet, 30, 31
reverse mortgages, 51, 58–59
    sample monthly payments, 59
    shopping for, 59
roommate, finding, 61
Roth IRAs, 129, 132–133
    converting 401(k)s into, 109
routine, missing, 11
RV living, 62

S

Savageau, David, 55, 65
savings, 126
    choosing from which to withdraw, 136
    for retirement, 21
    savings accounts, 126
scams, 48–49
    detecting, 49
scrapbooking, 77
second careers, 13, 78–79
    salary effect on Social Security
    payments, 99
Securities and Exchange Commission
    (SEC), 49
senility, 186
senior discounts, 34

senior living facilities, 61, 66–67
Senior Real Estate Specialists, 72
Senior Women's Travel, 85
Senior World Tours, 84
SEP IRAs, 114
    required minimum distributions (RMDs),
        114, 115
shared housing, 63
short-tem capital gain, 127
SIMPLE IRAs, 114
    early withdrawals, 115
    required minimum distributions (RMDs),
        114
Simplified Employee Pensions Plans.
        See SEP IRAs
*Single Best Source for Planning the Retirement
        You Deserve, The* (Savageau), 55
single-life annuity, 118–119
single premium deferred annuity, 134
smoking, 179
Social Security, 21, 90–103
    disability insurance, 101
    maximum income level, 103
    people not covered by, 102
    time to take, 95
    visit to local office, 97
Social Security benefits
    applying for, 96–97
    boosting, 99
    calculation, 92, 93
    direct deposit program, 102
    publications, 103
    reverse mortgage impact, 59
    salary effect on, 99
    and taxes, 33, 98–99
    widows, 102
    withholdings, 32
Special Olympics, 81
spending
    changes in, 22
    exceeding income, 26, 27

keeping track of, 22–23
    sample spending sheet, 23
spouse, 14–15, 16
    discussing will with, 163
    and estate taxes, 170
    and Social Security, 100
standard cost disclosure, 59
standard deduction, 33
states
    Medicaid and, 154
    state taxes, 33, 71
staying active, 74–90
stock market, 29
stocks, 127
    donating shares, 174
Susan G. Komen Breast Cancer Foundation, 81

T

T. Rowe Price, 30
taxes, 32–33
    bonds, 127
    capital gains, 174
    CDs, 126
    checking accounts, 126
    converting to a Roth IRA, 133
    deductibility of long-term care premiums,
        153, 156
    deferring payment with IRAs, 128
    estate taxes, 163, 170, 171, 174
    estimated quarterly payments, 32, 98
    estimating, 98
    home rental, 63
    home sale, 61
    401(k) and, 107
    money market accounts, 126
    money market mutual funds, 126
    moving, 70–71
    mutual funds, 127
    pensions, 117
    savings accounts, 126
    and seniors, 33

Social Security benefits and, 98–99
state taxes, 33, 71
stocks, 127
voluntary witholdings, 32, 98
tax executor, 170–171
Tax Reform Act (1986), 123
tenure reverse mortgage, 58
term life insurance, 140, 141
term reverse mortgage, 58
testator, 169
tetanus-diphtheria boosters, 185
total annual loan cost (TALC), 59
transition, gradual, 15, 16
Transitions Abroad, 62
transportation services for seniors, 88
traveling, 82–85
    disabled, 89
    and education, 84
    with a group, 84–85
    without partner, 88
trustee, 168, 169
trusts, 168–169

U

Uniform Distribution Period table
    (IRS Pub. 590), 130

V

variable annuity, 134, 135
vesting, 116, 117
    401(k)s, 107
Veterans' benefits, 33
Virtual Volunteering Project, 81
vision problems, 185
volunteer work, 80–81, 88
    volunteer travel programs, 83

W

Walking the World, 85
Web sites
    aaepa.com, 175
    aahsa.org, 73

aaii.org, 39
aarp.org, 17, 34, 59, 89, 193
aca.ch, 62
access-able.com, 89
acli.org, 157
aoa.dhhs.gov/factsheets/pension.html, 123
bankrate.com, 35, 43, 51
bestrate.com, 35, 43
bnuniversity.com, 87
career-planning.com, 89
ccaonline.org, 67
consumer.gov, 50
contwestins.com, 153
counselingforloss.com, 193
dealing with grief, 193
death-dying.com, 193
debtorsanonymous.org, 44
disabilitytravel.com, 89
disabilityworld.com, 89
earthwatch.org, 83
elderhostel.org, 83, 84
eldertreks.com, 85
estateweb.com, 175
fanniemae.com, 59
fnf.com, 153
fortnet.org/WidowNet, 193
fpanet.org/plannersearch/index.cfm, 37
Freedom.goGrrl.com, 89
ftc.gov, 39, 49, 50, 59
garrettplanningnetwork.com, 37
geocities.com/paris/1502, 89
globalvolunteers.org, 83
grandtrvi.com, 84–85
habitat.org, 81
homeexchange.com, 57
homelink.org, 57
homemods.org, 73
hudhcc.org, 59
hvousa.org, 83
icfa.org, 175
iesc.org, 83

independentliving.org/
vacationhomeswap.htm, 89

insure.com, 157

invest-faq.com, 39, 137

investoreducation.org, 39

IRAJunction.com, 137

irs.gov, 33, 130

johnhancock.com, 153

401k.com, 123

lifeadvice.com, 123

loanweb.com, 51

maillist.org/exercise, 183

malacainst-ch.es, 85

massmutual.com, 153

mayohealth.com, 193

medicare.gov, 157

money.com/money/depts/retirement/
bpretire, 65

myseniors.com, 89

nafep.com, 175

napfa.org, 37

nationalsharedhousing.org, 61

netplanning.com/consumer, 175

nolo.com/encyclopedia/ret_ency.html, 175

odysseys-unlimited.com, 85

othgi.com, 85

pbgc.gov, 121

photoexplorertours.com, 85

poshnosh.com, 85

pueblo.gsa.gov, 39

quicken.com, 30, 123

quicken.com/retirement, 39

quotesmith.com, 149

raceforthecure.com, 81

reseed.neu.edu, 87

retirementresorts.com, 62

reverse.org, 59

reversemortgage.org, 59

rivendell.org, 193

rvamerica.com, 62

seniorhousing.about.com, 65

SeniorHousing.net, 67

seniors.gov, 39

seniorsrealestate.com, 72

seniorworldtours.com, 84

serviceleader.org/vv, 81

smartmoney.com/estate, 175

smartmoney.com/retirement, 39

socialsecurity.com/opening.html, 103

specialolympics.org, 81

ssa.gov, 93, 103

ssa.gov/applytoretire, 96

50states.com, 73

toysfortots.org, 81

transitionsabroad.com, 62

travel-cruises.com, 89

troweprice.com, 30, 137

vanguard.com, 137

walkingtheworld.com, 85

walkingtours.com, 85

weight, 179

whole-life insurance, 140, 141

widows, 102

wills, 162–163

changes to, 165

as compared to living trusts, 169

overriden by beneficiary designations, 160

THE AUTHORS: UP CLOSE

Hope Egan is a certified financial planner as well as a certified public accountant. She has provided retirement, income tax, and investment guidance to individuals, small business owners, and large corporations, such as Ernst & Young and LaSalle National Trust. She was a contributing editor to **I Haven't Saved a Dime, Now What?!**

Barbara Wagner has written about retirement, debt—and yes, those dreaded budgets—for the past ten years. She recently wrote about "The Retirement Revolution" for Fidelity Investment's magazine for 401(k) participants. Her work has also appeared in *Business Week* and *Working Mother*, and she is the author of four consumer finance books, including a guide to 401(k)s and IRAs.

Barbara J. Morgan Publisher, Silver Lining Books

The *Now What?!* ™ series

Barb Chintz Editorial Director

Leonard Vigliarolo Design Director

I'm Retiring, Now What?! ™

Cinda Siler Editor

Robin Malik, Buddy Boy Design Graphic Design

Della R. Mancuso Production Manager

Marguerite Daniels Editorial Assistant

Picture Credits

Artville 15, 29, 30, 36, 37, 57, 60, 70, 94, 98, 106, 112, 128; **Comstock** 49; **Corbis** 80 Bob Krist; **Corbis Stock Market** cover (left) Ariel Skelley, cover (right) H. Armstrong Roberts; **Digital Stock** 4, 5, 11, 21, 26, 27, 32, 43, 53, 56, 61, 62, 64, 68, 76, 83, 87, 91, 101, 114, 125, 131, 139, 151, 159, 166, 168, 173, 177, 178, 180, 183, 186; **PhotoDisc** 7, 9, 12, 14, 19, 20, 24, 28, 35, 41, 42, 44, 46, 48, 54, 63, 75, 78, 84, 92, 93, 96, 97, 105, 108, 116, 127, 132, 134, 142, 154, 184; **Sally Mara Sturman** 1